Collins AQA GCSE Revision

Grade Booster

English
Language & Literature

Paul Burns

Contents

About this Book

This *AQA GCSE English Language and Literature Grade Booster* is for students who want to achieve the highest grades possible in their AQA English Language and Literature GCSE exams. If you have chosen this book, you are probably already confident that you can achieve good grades. This book will help you to transform those good grades into the highest grades.

By now you will have done all the hard work and acquired the skills you need to do well. For English Language, you should have practised critical analysis of both fiction and non-fiction texts as well as writing accurately and convincingly in a number of forms. For English Literature, you should know all your set books thoroughly and be able to write perceptively and critically about them. The skills you have learned through study of the set texts are transferable to unseen texts in both the Language and Literature exams.

People often say they find it difficult to revise for English. This is because it is a skill-based rather than a knowledge-based subject, so it is not a question of learning chunks of facts to regurgitate in the exam. For English Literature, there are some things that you can learn this way: you could learn some of the poems by heart, for example, memorise key quotations or make lists of key characters, themes and ideas to commit to memory. However, you also need plenty of practice and a thorough understanding of the requirements of the exams.

This book aims to help you maximise your existing skills in accordance with the requirements of the AQA exam board. Each chapter covers one section of an exam paper. It looks at the skills assessed for that section and reviews the main topics that you have studied. It also gives you a 'worked example', in which a typical question is considered with a reasonable (grade 4–5) answer and an improved (grade 7–9) answer. In this way you can get a clear idea of what is required to boost your performance to achieve the top grades.

Try to make active use of the worked examples. You could read the first sample answer and make notes on how it could be improved, compare your notes to the annotations, and then read the second sample and make notes on the ways in which it is better than the first. Alternatively, you could have a go at the question yourself before looking at the sample answers to see how they compare to your answer. You could then make notes on the ways in which you can improve your answer.

Top Tip boxes reinforce key points and give you handy hints to help you make those steps towards the highest grades. They also contain ideas for activities that will help you revise. Terms in **bold** are defined in the Glossary at the back of the book.

At the end of each chapter, you are signposted to pages in the *Collins AQA English Language & Literature Revision Guide* (ISBN 9780008112578) for more information on the topics covered. The same page references apply to the *Collins AQA English Language & Literature All-in-One Revision & Practice* book (ISBN 9780008112561).

The Examinations

English Language				English Literature		
Paper 1 – Explorations in Creative Reading and Writing	Section A (Reading): There will be four questions about an extract from a work of fiction.	40 marks		Paper 1 – Shakespeare and the 19th Century Novel	Section A (Shakespeare): There will be one question on each of six set plays.	34 marks
(1 hour 45 minutes)	Section B (Writing): There will be two tasks to choose from, one of them with a picture stimulus.	40 marks		(1 hour 45 minutes)	Section B (The 19th Century Novel): There will be one question on each of seven set novels.	30 marks
Paper 2 – Writers' Viewpoints and Perspectives	Section A (Reading): There will be four questions about two non-fiction texts.	40 marks		Paper 2 – Modern Texts and Poetry	Section A (Modern Prose or Drama): There will be a choice between two questions on each of the 12 set texts.	34 marks
(1 hour 45 minutes)	Section B (Writing): There will be one task, responding to a statement of opinion or responding to a viewpoint.	40 marks		(2 hours 15 minutes)	Section B (Poetry): There will be one question about poems from each of the two sections of the anthology.	30 marks
TOTAL		160 marks			Section C (Unseen Poetry): There will be two questions, the first about an unseen poem, and the second asking you to compare that poem with another unseen poem.	32 marks
				TOTAL		160 marks

Marking

The exams are marked externally by examiners who are trained to follow and apply the exam board's mark schemes. Sections of these mark schemes (slightly adapted for greater clarity) are reproduced throughout this book. You will notice that the exam board does not refer to grades 1–9 in its mark schemes. This is because grades are awarded for the subject as a whole, not for separate sections.

Grade thresholds are not decided until the exams have been marked. The thresholds differ from year to year – for example one year you might need 150 marks to gain a grade 9, while in another year it might be only 140. Therefore, for each question the marker awards a numerical mark within a level. Neither your teachers nor individual examiners can accurately predict what any given mark will mean in terms of grades. However, your teachers will do their best to give you a rough idea of what grade an answer might be approximately equivalent to – and so does this book. Each worked example in this book is assessed against the mark scheme and awarded a numerical mark within a level. An approximate equivalent grade is also given for your guidance. These are based on a comparison of the board's 'level descriptors' with guidance that the government has given on the requirements of different grades.

Luckily, as a reader of this Grade Booster, you do not have to worry about that. This book is all about striving for the highest grade – so all you have to do is try to reach the top end of the top level in almost every question you answer. Aim for consistency – with the occasional flash of genius!

2

English Language Paper 1

- Explorations in Creative Reading and Writing: Reading Literary Texts

The Exam

Paper 1 takes 1 hour and 45 minutes. You are advised to spend about 15 minutes reading the source material, which you will be given on a separate insert. This leaves you with 90 minutes, which you should divide equally between answering the reading questions and the writing question.

The source material will be taken from a work of literary fiction such as an extract from a novel or short story. Unless it is the complete text of a very short story, you will be told which part of the work it comes from, for example the opening or the ending. It will probably have been written in the 20th century. This may well be quite a well-known work, but if you happen to have read it, bear in mind that this is an 'unseen' exam so do not refer to anything that is not on your insert. There will only be one extract, so in this exam you will not be doing any comparison.

Skills Assessed in the Reading Section

The reading section of the exam assesses skills that you have been acquiring for most of your life: reading, understanding and evaluating. You have developed these skills in school, most recently by studying the set texts for your GCSE, but also more naturally through your own reading for pleasure. The best preparation for an exam such as this is to read widely, in as many forms and genres as you can, and to think about and discuss what you have read.

To revise for the reading part of the exam, you need to ensure that you understand what the examiners are asking you to do and practise doing it.

The Assessment Objectives you will be assessed on are:
- AO1 – identify and interpret explicit and implicit information and ideas
- AO2 – explain, comment on and analyse how writers use language and structure to achieve effects and influence their readers, using relevant subject terminology to support your views
- AO4 – evaluate the text critically and support this with appropriate textual references.

There will be four questions, each addressing a single Assessment Objective. In this chapter we will work through the reading section, using the kind of source material the exam board might use and looking at questions of the type that it would set. Read the text below before considering how to approach each question.

In the exam you might find it helpful to read the questions before the extract. You could then highlight or underline anything that you think might be relevant or that strikes you as interesting or worth commenting on in the text.

This extract is the opening of a novel by George Orwell. It was written in 1948 but set in the future (1984). Here, Orwell describes his protagonist, Winston Smith, arriving at Victory Mansions.

1984

It was a bright cold day in April, and the clocks were striking thirteen. Winston Smith, his chin nuzzled into his breast in an effort to escape the vile wind, slipped quickly through the glass doors of Victory Mansions, though not quickly enough to prevent a swirl of gritty dust from entering along with him.

The hallway smelt of boiled cabbage and old rag mats. At one end of it a coloured   5
poster, too large for indoor display, had been tacked to the wall. It depicted simply an
enormous face, more than a metre wide: the face of a man of about forty-five, with a heavy
black moustache and ruggedly handsome features. Winston made for the stairs. It was no
use trying the lift. Even at the best of times it was seldom working, and at present the electric
current was cut off during daylight hours. It was part of the economy drive in preparation for   10
Hate Week. The flat was seven flights up, and Winston, who was thirty-nine and had a
varicose ulcer above his right ankle, went slowly, resting several times on the way. On each
landing, opposite the lift shaft, the poster with the enormous face gazed from the wall. It was
one of those pictures which are so contrived that the eyes follow you about when you move.
BIG BROTHER IS WATCHING YOU, the caption beneath it ran.   15

Inside the flat a fruity voice was reading out a list of figures which had something to do
with the production of pig-iron. The voice came from an oblong metal plaque like a dulled
mirror which formed part of the surface of the right-hand wall. Winston turned a switch and
the voice sank somewhat, though the words were still distinguishable. The instrument (the
telescreen, it was called) could be dimmed, but there was no way of shutting it off   20
completely. He moved over to the window: a smallish, frail figure, the meagreness of his body
merely emphasized by the blue overalls which were the uniform of the Party. His hair was
very fair, his face naturally sanguine, his skin roughened by coarse soap and blunt razor
blades and the cold of the winter that had just ended.

Outside, even through the shut window-pane, the world looked cold. Down in the 25
street little eddies of wind were whirling dust and torn paper into spirals, and though the sun
was shining and the sky a harsh blue, there seemed to be no colour in anything, except the
posters that were plastered everywhere. The black-moustachio'd face gazed down from
every commanding corner. There was one on the house-front immediately opposite. BIG
BROTHER IS WATCHING YOU, the caption said, while the dark eyes looked deep into 30
Winston's own. Down at street level another poster, torn at one corner, flapped fitfully in the
wind, alternately covering and uncovering the single word INGSOC. In the far distance a
helicopter skimmed down beneath the roofs, hovering for an instant like a bluebottle, and
darted away again with a curving flight. It was the police patrol, snooping into people's
windows. The patrols did not matter, however. Only the Thought Police mattered. 35

Behind Winston's back the voice from the telescreen was still babbling away about pig-
iron and the overfulfilment of the Ninth Three-Year Plan. The telescreen received and
transmitted simultaneously. Any sound that Winston made, above the level of a very low
whisper, would be picked up by it; moreover, so long as he remained within the field of vision
which the metal plaque commanded, he could be seen as well as heard. There was of 40
course no way of knowing whether you were being watched at any given moment. How
often, or on what system, the Thought Police plugged in on any individual wire was
guesswork. It was even conceivable that they watched everybody all the time. But at any
rate they could plug in your wire whenever they wanted to. You had to live – did live,
from habit that became instinct – in the assumption that every sound you made was 45
overheard, and, except in darkness, every movement scrutinized.

Question 1

The first question addresses AO1 in its simplest form. It is designed to give you an
easy 'lead in' to the exam with a question that can be answered quickly and correctly
by the majority of candidates. It will probably ask you to list four things about a
particular aspect of the text. One mark will be awarded for each item correctly
identified. Answers can be direct quotation or **paraphrases**.

You are being asked to 'identify' information and possibly ideas but not to 'interpret'
them. The information will probably be explicit rather than implicit, so you will not
be doing a lot of inferring from the text, except perhaps in the most straightforward
way. The biggest dangers for high-achieving candidates in this question are spending
too much time on it and not reading the question properly.

Worked Example

See page 3 for suggestions on how to make effective use of worked examples.

1 Read again the first part of the source, from line 1 to line 15. List four things from this part of the text that you learn about Victory Mansions.   [4 marks]

If you re-read the first 15 lines of the extract from *1984,* you should find more than four possible answers. You could have any four from:
- *There are glass doors.*
- *There is a large poster at the end of the hallway* or *There is a poster of a man with a moustache.*
- *The hallway smells of boiled cabbage and old rag mats* or *There is a smell of boiled cabbage* or *There is a smell of old rag mats in the hall.*
- *There are at least seven flights of stairs.*
- *On each floor there is a poster opposite the lift shaft.*
- *The lift is not working* or just *There is a lift.*

You can use different wording, and may quote directly from the text, but keep your answers short and do not express a point of view. There are pitfalls, however, and here are some examples of wrong answers:

The clock strikes thirteen.

You are not told that the clocks are in or anywhere near Victory Mansions; it is a general observation.

Winston Smith lives there.

You might reasonably **infer** this but at this stage you cannot be sure: he could be visiting someone.

There are seven flights of stairs.

The flat is seven flights up so you can safely infer that there are at least seven but you do not know whether there are only seven or more than seven.

There is a telescreen in the flat.

This information comes after the section specified in the question.

> *The flat was seven flights up, and Winston, who was thirty-nine and had a varicose ulcer above his right ankle, went slowly, resting several times on the way.*

This is mostly about Winston, not the building. Somewhere in there lurks the information that there are at least seven flights but it is not clear to the examiner that this is what you have learned.

Here is an example of an answer that is not wrong but is unnecessarily long:

> *We know that the lift is not working because there 'was no use trying' it because 'even at the best of times it was seldom working, and at present the electric current was cut off during daylight hours'.*

You would probably still get a mark for this because you have identified the fact that there is a lift that does not work but there is no need to include the explanation of how you have worked this out or why the lift is not working.

Top Tip

Read the question, do what it tells you and keep it short. It is as simple as that. But remember, there are 4 marks for this question, which is 10% of the total marks for the paper and 5% of the marks for the whole exam. Those marks could be the difference between two grades, so make sure you get them.

Question 2

Question 2 focuses on language. Like question 1 it will direct you to a specific part of the text and you should ensure that you limit your answer to that section, taking all quotations from it. The mark scheme is based on AO2 only. This asks you to <u>explain, comment on and analyse</u> how writers use language to <u>achieve effects and influence readers</u>. Average candidates would be expected to be able to explain, but only the best will analyse. In commenting on language, you must show that you understand not only what the writer is doing but what the effect is. In reading fiction, you will be thinking more about achieving effects than influencing readers. You must also use <u>relevant subject terminology</u> to support your views.

Look at the following sentence:

> Before such calm external beauty the presence of a vague fear is more distinctly felt – like a raven flapping its slow wing across the sunny air.
>
> *(From Silas Marner by George Eliot)*

Think about the effect of this sentence on you, the reader. Does it make you feel uneasy, worried, perhaps even frightened? In this case, you do not know the context but you can assume that a beautiful scene has been described, so there is a sense of happiness and calm coming to an end.

How does the writer achieve this effect? First, there is the contrast between 'calm… beauty' and 'a vague fear'. Then, she uses a striking **simile** to express this fear in visual terms.

A reasonably good student might explain the effect by writing:

> *The writer makes the reader feel uneasy and worried about what might happen[1] by contrasting[2] 'calm external beauty' with 'a vague fear'.[3] Then she uses the simile[4] of a raven flying 'across the sunny air' to make what she has said more real.[5]*

[1] This is a clear description of the effect on a reader.
[2] 'Contrasting' counts as appropriate terminology.
[3] Two short quotations used effectively.
[4] Appropriate subject terminology.
[5] An attempt, albeit a vague one, to explain the reason for using a simile.

The student has clearly explained the use of language and its effect on the reader, and has used some appropriate subject terminology. There is nothing wrong with this answer but if you want to achieve the highest grades you need to <u>analyse</u> – that means more depth and more detail. This is a better answer:

> *The writer starts with a generalisation about the effect of a contrast between the external world and someone's feelings, the juxtaposition[1] of 'calm… beauty' and 'vague fear'[2] creating tension and a sense of anxiety.[3] She breaks the sentence with a dash, making us pause and giving more impact to the simile that follows.[4] Ravens are often associated with death.[5] The raven blocks out the sun by 'flapping its slow wing'. This sounds slow and heavy, reflecting the depressing, uneasy feeling of the vague fear referred to earlier.[6]*

English Language Paper 1

[1] 'Generalisation' and 'juxtaposition' are both examples of appropriate terminology. Beware of the word 'juxtaposition'. It just means putting two things together, not necessarily contrasting things. It is used properly here as 'contrast' is also mentioned.

[2] Appropriate use of embedded quotations.

[3] Clear linkage of the technique and its effect.

[4] Punctuation is part of language but its effect can be difficult to analyse.

[5] When writing about imagery consider the **connotations** of the **image** used. Why a raven and not just 'a bird'?

[6] Links the sounds used and sentiments expressed.

Worked Example

2 Look in detail at this extract from lines 16 to 24 of the source.

> Inside the flat a fruity voice was reading out a list of figures which had something to do with the production of pig-iron. The voice came from an oblong metal plaque like a dulled mirror which formed part of the surface of the right-hand wall. Winston turned a switch and the voice sank somewhat, though the words were still distinguishable. The instrument (the telescreen, it was called) could be dimmed, but there was no way of shutting it off **20** completely. He moved over to the window: a smallish, frail figure, the meagreness of his body merely emphasized by the blue overalls which were the uniform of the Party. His hair was very fair, his face naturally sanguine, his skin roughened by coarse soap and blunt razor blades and the cold of the winter that had just ended.

How does the writer use language here to describe the sort of life led by Winston Smith?

You could include the writer's choice of:
- words and phrases
- language features and techniques
- sentence forms. [8 marks]

The passage is very short, which indicates that the examiners are looking for very detailed analysis. The bullet points indicate that you should:
- select and comment on any words and phrases that strike you as interesting and contribute to the overall impression you get of Winston Smith's life
- comment on any particular linguistic techniques that are used, for example **imagery, alliteration, onomatopoeia, rhetorical questions** and **hyperbole**
- comment on sentence forms, for example **compound sentences, complex sentences, minor sentences**, questions and imperatives.

> **Top Tip**
>
> To get high marks you must ensure that you cover all three of these bullet points. For example, if you do not make any comments on sentence forms (the point that is probably the easiest to overlook), you could lose up to a third of the marks.

The examiners' mark scheme says that to gain a very high mark you need to:
- show a detailed and perceptive understanding of language
- analyse the effects of the writer's choice of language
- select a judicious range of relevant quotations
- use sophisticated subject terminology.

That all sounds marvellous, but what do they actually mean by 'perceptive', 'judicious' and 'sophisticated'? How is this different from a mid-range answer, where you should:
- clearly explain the effects of the language
- use a range of relevant quotations
- use subject terminology clearly and accurately?

Sample Answer 1

Let's look at a reasonably good answer and see how it can be improved.

> *The first part of the paragraph describes the flat and what is happening in it. It makes it sound dull and depressing. The sentences are all quite long.[1] The news is 'something to do with the production of pig-iron'. The vagueness of the phrase 'something to do with' implies it cannot be interesting and 'pig-iron' sounds both boring and unpleasant.[2] He goes on to use words like 'dulled', 'sank' and 'dimmed', which all add to a sense of depression.[3] This tells us that Winston's life cannot be very interesting or enjoyable.[4] Then he describes Winston himself. We get a picture of his appearance from a list of physical features.[5] The noun 'meagreness' and the adjective 'frail' emphasise that he is weak and maybe not well.[6] The writer does not comment on his character but details like 'coarse soap and blunt razor blades' suggest that he is poor and life is hard for him.[7]*

[1] The candidate mentions sentence structure but without any explanation of its effect. As there is nothing obviously striking or unusual about the sentence structure in this passage, it is difficult to comment on.

[2] This is better. Appropriate quotations are used and their effect explained. The candidate is starting to analyse language.

[3] Good use of one-word quotations. 'Words', like 'sentences' and 'paragraph', is subject terminology at its most basic level.
[4] A good explanation of the effect of the use of these words on the reader.
[5] 'A list' is appropriate subject terminology. It describes the structure of the sentence and its effect is described in simple terms.
[6] 'Noun' and 'adjective' are used correctly and the candidate explains the effect of their use.
[7] A good explanation of how the use of detail helps to give us a picture of Winston's life.

The answer shows understanding of the way language is used. It is not always focused on the question but does eventually address it directly, linking the use of language to our impression of Winston Smith's life. Quotations from the text are used well and some subject terminology is used. Although there is not much on sentence structure, the candidate does select and comment on words and phrases that contribute to our impression of Winston. There are not many obvious literary techniques used in this passage, so it is a difficult area, but the candidate manages to say something about the list and the use of details.

Mark 5 / 8 (Level 3, equivalent to approx. grade 5)

Sample Answer 2

Let's see what can be changed and added to lift the answer to the next level.

At the start of the paragraph, the 'fruity' voice reading the news strikes an odd note. The voice seems at odds with what it is reading: 'something to do with the production of pig-iron'. The vagueness of this phrase implies it is of little interest to Winston and 'pig-iron' sounds both boring and unpleasant.[1] An atmosphere of dullness and depression is created by the use of vocabulary such as 'dulled', 'sank' and 'dimmed'. All these words are used here in a literal sense but are associated with a state of mind.[2]

The writer uses the adjectives 'smallish' and 'frail' and the noun 'meagreness' to describe Winston, creating a picture of physical weakness, which is 'emphasized' by his uniform.[3] The uniform implies a lack of individuality and the capital letter at the beginning of 'Party' indicates its importance and power, in contrast with Winston's weakness.[4] Details like 'coarse soap and blunt razor blades' suggest that he is poor and life is hard for him, and the reference to 'the cold winter' shows that he is at the mercy of forces he cannot control.[5]

The paragraph consists of complex sentences of roughly equal length, which enable the writer to give a measured and detailed description of Winston and his flat.[6] Writing in the third person, the writer does not 'let us in' to Winston's mind and there is a sense of detachment,[7] underlined by the lack of rhetorical devices or figurative imagery (although the description of the room might be seen as pathetic fallacy, reflecting his mood).[8] The detailed literal imagery, however, effectively conveys Winston's powerlessness and the rather dull, restricted life he leads.[9]

[1] This candidate makes the same point as the first, but it is more detailed and links the quotations more effectively with the focus of the question and the effect on the reader.

[2] Again, the same point is made but the candidate here analyses the use of the words and their effect.

[3] The candidate goes into a bit more detail and is clear about the effect of the language. 'Noun' and 'adjective' are used correctly.

[4] This is a perceptive point which many candidates would miss.

[5] The previous answer has made the same point but this candidate goes a little further with a perceptive comment about a phrase that others might not have considered important.

[6] Correct terminology and a very good attempt to describe the effect of sentence structure.

[7] It is always worth commenting on the narrative voice and how it is used. This is becoming quite sophisticated.

[8] The candidate has noticed the lack of obvious literary techniques to discuss but cleverly manages to comment on that very lack. The comment on pathetic fallacy is measured and thoughtful, showing a real understanding of how literary devices are used.

[9] The final sentence, again, shows an advanced understanding of literary technique and effectively sums up the effect sought by the writer.

There is a lot more detail in this answer. The candidate often uses the same material but the comments move from explanation to analysis. There are also comments on things that the first candidate has not spotted. The candidate has a very secure knowledge and understanding of how language is used and always keeps in mind its effect. It is analytical and perceptive, there is a range of quotations – you could say a 'judicious' range as they are sensibly chosen – and the terminology used is as sophisticated as you could expect. It should get full marks.

Mark 8 / 8 (Level 4, equivalent to approx. grade 8–9)

> **Top Tip**
>
> Literal imagery is simply the use of description, often to convey mood or atmosphere.
>
> Figurative imagery is the use of an image of one thing to tell us about something else. This includes metaphors, similes and personification.
>
> If there is no figurative imagery in the passage, you can always comment on the literal imagery.

Question 3

Question 3 focuses on structure. You will be asked to write about the whole of the source. The mark scheme for this question is also based on AO2. This time you are expected to <u>explain, comment on and analyse</u> how writers use <u>structure</u> to <u>achieve effects</u> and influence readers. As with question 2, the strongest candidates will be expected to go beyond explanation to analysis. Again, you must focus on the effect on the reader and use <u>relevant subject terminology</u> to support your views.

It is important to be clear about what is meant by structure. In this context, structure refers to how texts are ordered and organised. In your answer to question 2, you should already have discussed sentence structure. Now you are looking at something bigger.

When studying a novel, short story or play you may have considered story structure. Most stories are organised in a similar way, starting with **exposition**, followed by an **inciting incident**, one or more turning points, a **climax** and a **denouement** (this will be discussed more fully in the Literature section of this book). Unless you are presented with a complete short story (which is unlikely), you will be unable to analyse the structure of the whole story in answering this question.

However, you should show that you are aware of the extract's place in the novel or story as a whole. You do not have to work this out for yourself because at the beginning of the source you will be told where the extract comes from. For example:
- This text is from the opening of a novel.
- This text is an important turning point in a novel.
- This text comes from the ending of a novel.

The first of these is the most likely. If the text is from the beginning of a story, you might think it appropriate to mention exposition and its purpose:

> *Having introduced the protagonist in the first paragraph, the writer continues his exposition with a description of the house where she lives.*

Similarly, if you are told that the extract is from near the end:

> *When the detective gathers the other characters together in one room, it is clear the writer is building up to the denouement when the identity of the murderer will be revealed.*

However, you should not dwell on this because the main purpose of the question is to test whether you can effectively analyse how the extract itself is structured – which might seem rather artificial as the passage was never intended to be seen as an entity with its own structure. Nevertheless, that is your task, so let's look at the sort of question that might be asked and think about how best to answer it.

Worked Example

3 You now need to think about the whole of the source.

This text is the opening of a novel.

How has the writer structured the text to interest you as a reader?

You could write about:
- what the writer focuses your attention on at the beginning
- how and why the writer changes this focus as the source develops
- any other structural features that interest you.   [8 marks]

You can see from the first two bullet points that the examiners want you to write about the writer's focus, that is, what is being written about. They want you to point out when, how and why this focus changes. It may change once, twice or even more during the passage. A change of subject might be signalled by the start of a new paragraph. It may change focus from character to setting or vice versa. It could change focus from one character to another or one scene to another. It could move from description to dialogue or to interior monologue, conveying the thoughts and feelings of a character. You might notice a sudden shift in mood or tone.

In the third bullet point you are asked to write about 'any other structural features that interest you'. You should not discuss sentence structure in detail as this was covered in the last question. You might consider:
- paragraph length – perhaps their length varies, with occasional short ones for effect
- links between paragraphs, 'signposting' and topic sentences
- structure within a paragraph
- use of **direct speech**
- patterns created by repetition or **motifs**
- any variations on **chronological order**.

> ### Top Tip
>
> The key to answering the structure question is not to over-complicate it in your mind. It's all about structure at paragraph level and how the narrative develops.
>
> Work your way through the passage a paragraph at a time, keeping an eye open for anything unusual.

Sample Answer 1

Here is a reasonable attempt at a difficult question:

The first paragraph starts with a surprising statement, which captures the reader's interest: 'the clocks were striking thirteen'. It then quickly introduces the protagonist, Winston Smith, and describes the weather.[1] The other paragraphs are much longer.[2] The second moves the focus to inside 'Victory Mansions' and describes what it is like as it tells us about what Winston is doing.[3] Attention is drawn to the slogan 'BIG BROTHER IS WATCHING YOU' by the capital letters.[4] In the third paragraph we move into the flat. The first part of it tells us about the flat, giving more of an idea about the world that is being described. The writer moves on to describe Winston so we now have a picture of him and his surroundings.[5]

The fourth paragraph starts 'outside', contrasting with 'inside', the first word of the previous paragraph.[6] Now we get a description of the environment around the building, which is just as depressing. The poster is mentioned again, and again the slogan is in capitals, emphasising its importance.[7] The paragraph builds to a sense of danger and menace with the final sentence 'Only the Thought Police mattered'. The reader will want to know what is meant by the Thought Police and learn more about the strange world that Winston lives in.[8]

In the last paragraph the writer turns back to the inside of the flat and brings our attention back to the telescreen. Now he explains how it works, leading us to an understanding of what the Thought Police are and how they work. At first it focuses on Winston but it becomes clear that it is the same for everyone.

[1] This addresses the first bullet point and shows awareness of the passage being the opening of a novel and the need to interest the reader and introduce characters.

[2] A brief comment on paragraph length though without any comment about its effect.

[3] Addresses the second bullet point – awareness of how the focus changes.

[4] An unusual or unexpected feature – the use of capitals – has been noticed and its effect commented on (third bullet point).

[5] Back to the second bullet point, implying an understanding of exposition – 'a picture of him and his surroundings'. The candidate had also noted the shift of subject matter within the paragraph.

[6] Comment on how paragraphs are linked (third bullet point).

[7] The candidate has noticed the repetition and the importance of the poster.

[8] Comment on how the writer builds tension within the paragraph.

This is a very creditable attempt and successfully explains how the passage is structured. The first two bullet points have been covered, with a clear explanation of how the focus shifts from one paragraph to another. As requested by the third bullet point, the candidate has found some other structural features to comment on. There are a few relevant quotations – we would not really expect as many as in an answer that focuses on language. Subject terminology, although limited (paragraphs, **protagonist**, slogan), is used appropriately.

Mark 5 / 8 (Level 3, equivalent to approx. grade 5)

Sample Answer 2

Now let's look at an answer that moves from explanation to analysis, uses an appropriate range of quotations, and uses sophisticated subject terminology.

The passage starts with a statement which captures the reader's interest: 'the clocks were striking thirteen'. This is disturbing as well as intriguing. The rest of this short opening paragraph introduces the protagonist, Winston Smith, and briefly describes the environment.[1]

As the exposition continues, paragraphs are much longer, allowing us to learn about the protagonist, the 'world' of the novel and his place in it.[2] The second moves the focus to inside 'Victory Mansions' as Winston himself moves into the building.[3] Our attention is drawn to the large poster. Its significance is emphasised both by the writer returning to it at the end of the paragraph and by the capital letters of the slogan 'BIG BROTHER IS WATCHING YOU'.[4]

In the third paragraph we (and Winston) move into the flat. The first part of it tells us about the flat itself, giving more of an idea about the drab yet disturbing world of 1984. The writer moves on to describe Winston, so linking this 'frail' figure with his depressing and oppressive environment.[5]

The next paragraph starts 'outside', contrasting with 'inside', the first word of the previous paragraph. 'Outside' is described as Winston sees it through the window. We are beginning to share Winston's experience.[6] After a description of a world in which 'there seemed to be no colour in anything' the writer again describes the poster and its slogan, which has now become a motif.[7] Then the mood changes with the sight of the helicopter, creating a sense of danger and menace which reaches a climax with the final, short sentence, 'Only the Thought Police mattered'.[8]

The fifth paragraph begins by referring back to the voice from the telescreen, and ties this together with the sinister police of the previous paragraph.[9] The writer now explains how the Thought Police operate and ends with a sense of how life must be for everybody, not just Winston, as indicated by the use of 'you'.

[1] This consideration of the first bullet point is more explicit in showing that the candidate understands how the opening affects the reader.
[2] Here there is some understanding of why paragraphs may differ in length and a use of terminology ('protagonist', 'exposition') which we could judge to be sophisticated.
[3] Addressing the second bullet point, the candidate analyses how the writer changes the focus.
[4] The candidate mentions an unusual or unexpected feature – the use of capitals – as well as analysing the internal structure of the paragraph.
[5] Comment on the shift of focus between the paragraphs and how the shift of focus within it works to connect the protagonist and his world.
[6] Comment on how paragraphs are linked (third bullet point) and a perceptive comment about how the writer is gradually letting us into the protagonist's thoughts.
[7] A good analysis of how focus and mood shift within the paragraph. Correct use of the term 'motif'.
[8] Comment on how the writer builds tension within the paragraph.
[9] Links between the paragraphs.

There is much more analysis here. The candidate goes beyond a consideration of how things change from paragraph to paragraph and considers structure within paragraphs. The use of subject terminology is secure and there are several appropriate quotations, with comments always rooted firmly in the text.

Mark ▸ **7 / 8 (Level 4, equivalent to approx. grade 7)**

Question 4

The final question of the reading section carries half the total marks and, therefore, you should spend between 20 and 25 minutes on it. You might expect it to be about the whole text but, like the first two questions, it asks you to focus on part of the text – so ensure that you only refer to the specified section in your answer.

This question is judged against AO4, which requires that you <u>evaluate the text critically</u> and support this with <u>appropriate textual reference</u>. The exam board says it is looking for a personal judgement that is informed and supported by reference to the text. It also wants 'a degree of detachment'. At first sight this seems contradictory. To most people, evaluating something means saying whether you think it has any value. Making a 'personal judgement' means something similar and neither usually involves being 'detached'. However, in 'exam speak', evaluation means close analysis combined with an 'overview' of a text, that is, not simply looking at details but showing an understanding of how details contribute to the whole. You are allowed to give opinions but not on the level of:

Personally, I think this is a terrible text. Mary is a very unsympathetic character and I was glad when she fell off the horse.

Or the rather sycophantic:

Brown's use of adjectives is superb. I really identify with Mary and I think the bit where she falls off the horse is the most moving piece of prose I have ever read.

These views are perfectly valid, of course, and could be recast as thus:

Mary's constant references to how she is 'a poor starved little creature' and her 'cruel and unfeeling father' might be designed to invoke sympathy from other characters and even from the reader but, in my view, they make Snedwell's reaction to her accident understandable and many readers would join him in urging her to 'get back on the 'orse and pull yerself together'.

Or:

> *Brown's use of adjectives such as 'frail' and 'delicate' give a picture of someone who needs protecting. The journey is seen from her point of view, making the reader empathise with her. Although the accident is seen as trivial and even comic by the other characters, the description of Mary's pain and embarrassment vividly conveys what it means to her.*

In the latter two answers, there is a sense of the reader being a little detached, partly because of the absence of phrases such as 'I think' but also because of a lack of hyperbole ('superb') and the presence of evidence from the text, in the form of quotations. Nevertheless, personal views are expressed.

Worked Example

 Focus this part of your answer on the second part of the source from line 25 to the end.

A student who has read this part of the text said: 'The writer has created a vision of a future world that is both bleak and frightening.'

To what extent do you agree?

In your response, you could:
- write about your own impressions of the world Orwell describes
- evaluate how he has created these impressions
- support your opinions with references to the text.   [20 marks]

The first thing to note about this question is that it begins with the opinion of a (probably fictional) student. This statement gives you the focus for your question and it is of vital importance that you keep to this focus throughout your answer.

The student's opinion is followed by the question: 'To what extent do you agree?' The use of the phrase 'to what extent' is important because it invites you to evaluate. It is not just a question of whether you agree or not. You may whole-heartedly agree, you may agree with reservations or you may think the 'student' has got the wrong end of the stick completely. Be warned, though: the last of these is highly unlikely.

As ever, you must pay attention to the bullet points. The first asks you to show your understanding of the text by saying just what your impressions are, using your skills of inference and deduction. In the second, the key word is 'how', a word that includes the writer's use of language and structure. You should think about the intended effect of the writer's methods.

Finally, you are reminded to support your opinions with references to the text – something you have been doing in the previous two questions.

 Top Tip

This question is all about evaluating the effect of the writing on the reader. You are the reader.

Examiners love you to use lots of very short quotations 'embedded' in your answer.

For a top answer (Level 4) you are expected to show 'perceptive and detailed evaluation', while for a Level 3 answer you need 'clear, relevant evaluation'.

Sample Answer 1

Let's look at an answer that would come within Level 3 and see how it can be improved.

I think the statement is largely true. Although it is not terrifying, like a horror story, the idea of what it must be like living in this world is worrying and scary but it also sounds quite boring.[1]

When Winston looks out of the window he sees a world that is very ordinary. The writer mentions the weather and says 'the world looked cold', implying he means more than just the actual temperature.[2] The world is unwelcoming and dull. The 'dust and torn paper' make me think of a neglected place and when he says 'there seemed to be no colour' you think of an old-fashioned black and white film, not a future world, which you might expect to be shiny and exciting. Instead this is just dull.[3] It is not frightening but the description of the poster makes you wonder who this 'big brother' is and why he is watching 'from every commanding corner'. His 'black moustachio'd face' suggests he is not friendly and no-one likes being watched all the time, so you might be a bit frightened.[4] Then the helicopter, compared in a simile to 'a bluebottle', turns up 'snooping into people's windows'. This sounds very sinister but the writer says it does 'not matter'.[5] The short sentence 'Only the Thought Police mattered' is what makes you start to feel scared. We do not know what is meant by this but it implies the police can read your thoughts and that if you think the wrong thing you could be arrested or worse.

> *The tension drops in the next paragraph and the writer describes the telescreen in a calm way, just explaining how it works. He does not use scary words or exaggerate so he does not seem to be trying to frighten the reader.[6] He just seems to be telling us about how life is in the future. The voice 'babbling away about pig-iron' just sounds really uninteresting. If this is what's on the television, the future must be really dull and bleak.[7] The fact that Winston 'could be seen as well as heard' is worrying but it does not frighten Winston. It is as if you just have to learn to live with it: 'you had to live… in the assumption that every sound you made was overheard…every movement scrutinized.' The thought of this does send shivers up my spine. It is frightening to think you are being watched all the time. However, the writer does not describe Winston as being scared. He seems to have learned to live with it, which itself is worrying. I would say this future certainly looks bleak but it is not so much frightening as depressing.[8]*

[1] The candidate is addressing the question in a general way.

[2] Starting to show an appreciation of the writer's method.

[3] Clear evaluative comment, focused on the question and supported by textual reference.

[4] Clear reference to the effect on the reader.

[5] Focus on the question, with clear understanding of the writer's use of language and effective use of several quotations.

[6] Clear evaluation of the writer's probable intentions linked to his methods.

[7] Personal opinion linked to the question.

[8] Good attempt at responding to the statement. The candidate considers both parts – 'frightening' and 'bleak' and expresses a clear personal view, rooted in the evidence.

This is an honest attempt to give a clear response to the statement. Throughout the answer the candidate considers whether the world Orwell describes is frightening and/or bleak, coming to a reasoned conclusion that 'frightening' is possibly over-stating the case but 'bleak' is accurate. An understanding of the writer's methods is shown with references to language, structure and tone. There is a range of references and they are all relevant. There is not enough detail or analysis to take the answer into Level 4 but it does everything required at Level 3.

Mark ▶ **14 / 20 (Level 3, equivalent to approx. grade 5)**

Top Tip

Throughout your answer, refer to the statement you have been asked to discuss.

Sample Answer 2

Now let's see how it can be transformed into an answer that might get into Level 4.

I think the statement is true to a great extent. The text is not frightening in the sense that a horror story might be frightening but, like many science fiction stories, it paints a picture of a dystopian world, which is certainly bleak and oppressive and possibly also frightening.[1]

The scene described from Winston's point of view as he looks through the window is not noticeably different from today's world. Referring back to the previous paragraph, the writer says 'the world looked cold' and describes the sky as being a 'harsh blue'. The adjectives 'cold' and 'harsh' are used figuratively as well as literally, hinting that the whole world is cold and harsh. The 'dust and torn paper' give the impression of a bleak urban landscape and 'there seemed to be no colour' implies a lack of variety and a lack of joy. A monochrome world is a bleak world. The fact that the only colour is in the poster of big brother emphasises how it – and he – dominates the scene.[2]

The idea of 'big brother' might have lost the impact it would have had to early readers of this novel but the description of the poster is still disturbing. It makes you wonder who this 'big brother' is and why he is watching 'from every commanding corner'.[3] 'Commanding' is a transferred epithet as it is not the corner that is commanding but Big Brother himself. He is clearly a figure of authority. His 'black moustachio'd face' suggests he is not a benign authority figure – these are the looks of a traditional villain – yet the use of the word 'gazed' takes away some of the menace. However, his 'dark eyes looked deep into Winston's own', which is at least unnerving, if not actually frightening.[4]

Any ambiguity about authority is destroyed by Orwell's description of the police helicopter. Today we are used to hearing and seeing the 'eye in the sky' but the writer makes it clear that this helicopter, compared to 'a bluebottle', an irritating unpleasant insect, is not welcome. It is 'snooping into people's windows', suggesting a nosy neighbour. This might just be irritating but the next two short sentences make it sound more sinister – something potentially to be feared.[5] It does 'not matter' suggests that people are desensitised to this level of interference but then we find out what does matter. 'Only the Thought Police'. This statement is chilling. What is the Thought Police? Can they read your thoughts? What will they do to you if they don't like what you're thinking? A world where this can happen must be a frightening place to live.[6]

The tension drops in the next paragraph as the writer describes the telescreen in a calm way. He does not use emotive adjectives or hyperbole so he does not seem to be trying to frighten the reader.[7] He just seems to be telling us about how life is in 1984 – dull and boring when instead of entertainment you get someone 'babbling away about pig-iron'. If this is what's on the television, the future must be bleak.[8] The writer goes on to tell us that Winston 'could be seen as well as heard'. This is disturbing and you might expect Winston to be frightened but it seems it is just part of life: 'you had to live... in the assumption that every sound you made was overheard...every movement scrutinized.' Winston may not seem bothered by this but it makes the reader think about what might happen to him.[9] The idea of the authorities having so much power is frightening. It does not make me feel frightened in an emotional way, as it does not describe immediate danger or describe anything that is obviously frightening, but rather in a thoughtful way – frightened about what the future might hold.[10]

[1] The candidate addresses the question in a general way, showing an impressive grasp of the text's **genre**.

[2] A detailed evaluation of the writer's methods, supported by well-chosen quotations.

[3] Focused on the reader.

[4] Perceptive comments clearly related to the statement and sophisticated use of subject terminology.

[5] Critical evaluation of the effect on the reader.

[6] Critical response, linking reader's reaction to the statement.

[7] Consideration of the writer's methods related to speculation about his intention.

[8] Personal reaction but focused on the statement.

[9] Critical evaluation – the candidate considers whether the character is frightened and whether the reader might be frightened.

[10] The last sentence effectively sums up the candidate's response to the statement.

This answer analyses detail well and relates the detail to the whole. The statement is constantly kept in mind. Is this vision of the future frightening? Is it bleak? The response to these questions is nuanced and convincingly argued, well supported by evidence from the text.

Mark ▶ **20 / 20 (Level 4, equivalent to approx. grade 9)**

 For more on the topics covered in this chapter, see pages 36–39 of the Collins AQA English Language & Literature Revision Guide.

Skills Assessed in the Writing Section

You will have about 45 minutes to produce a piece of creative writing, either narrative (a story or part of a story) or descriptive writing. There will be a choice of two tasks, one of which will include a picture stimulus. You may have a choice between narrative and descriptive writing but it is also possible that both tasks could be narrative or both descriptive, so it is important that you feel comfortable with both types of writing.

The Assessment Objectives you will be assessed on are:
- AO5 – communicate clearly, effectively and imaginatively, selecting and adapting tone, style and register for different forms, purposes and audiences. Organise information and ideas, using structural and grammatical features to support coherence and cohesion of texts.
- AO6 – use a range of vocabulary and sentence structures for clarity, purpose and effect, with accurate spelling and punctuation.

The two AOs are assessed separately, AO5 as 'Content and Organisation' and AO6 as 'Technical Accuracy'. The first of these carries 24 marks and the second carries 16 marks.

 Top Tip

Before you start writing, spend about five minutes planning your answer, focusing especially on the structure of the piece.

Content and Organisation

'Content' does not refer to your subject matter except insofar as you are expected to write about whatever the question specifies and not just something that takes your fancy. It refers to whether your writing is suitable for its purpose and audience and to your use of language.

For this paper you do not have to think too carefully about purpose and audience. The purpose of creative writing will always be the same – to entertain and interest the reader. A less general purpose might be given in the question, for example 'you are entering a creative writing competition' but this makes little difference. After all, how would writing for a competition be any different from writing for an exam or writing for publication? Similarly, an audience could be specified, for example 'a magazine for people of your own age' but, again, this makes little difference. Just write for an intelligent person of at least your own age. Or for yourself.

The 'tone, style and **register**' you are aiming for here are the tone, style and register that suit you. You might want to amuse your readers, maybe using a detached **ironic** style or an enthusiastic jokey style. You might want to adopt the style and tone of a horror story, using atmospheric description and heightening tension. Or you could write a gentle, even sombre piece on a sad theme.

'Register' refers to the sort of language you use and, as with tone and style, this question gives you the opportunity to write in the register that you think is right for your subject matter. In a third person narrative you would be expected to write in **Standard English** but if your narrative is first person, you should write in the voice appropriate to the narrator. What sort of tone would that person use? Would he or she use **dialect** or **slang**? Using non-standard English throughout your piece might seem risky as Standard English is mentioned in the mark scheme, but if not using it is obviously a deliberate choice, you should not lose out. If you're worried, perhaps you could use a mixture of Standard and non-standard English, for example using two 'voices', one 'framing' the other. You might want to use non-standard forms in direct speech to make your characters come to life. Direct speech can be useful both to tell us about character and to advance the story, but use it sparingly. Think about whether it adds anything and set it out correctly. Sometimes **indirect** (or reported) **speech** is more effective.

The other part of the 'content' mark is for using extensive and ambitious vocabulary and well-crafted linguistic devices. The danger in thinking too much about this is that you could end up using pretentious or obscure vocabulary, not always correctly, instead of the words that express what you want to say. Good creative writing can be moving, funny, quirky or challenging. But it is not forced.

Top Tip

Your task is to write creatively and with imagination. It is your chance to spread your wings and be original.

To develop an extensive vocabulary, keep a notebook. Whenever you come across a new word (or one you are not sure about), look it up in the dictionary and then enter it in your notebook with a brief definition and an example of how it is used.

'Organisation' is all about the structure of your work. At the most basic level this means writing in paragraphs and linking your ideas. The best candidates' paragraphs are fluently linked and their writing is 'compelling' because it is structured in such a way as to draw in readers and keep them interested.

Narrative Writing

Read the task carefully. You might be asked to write a complete short story but you are just as likely to be asked to write part of one – probably the opening.

Think first about voice. Are you going to write in the first or the third person? If you choose first person, is the narrator you (or a version of you) or an invented character? Is he or she the protagonist of the story or an observer?

If writing in the third person you can be an **omniscient narrator**, who can read the thoughts of your characters, or you can be more detached and just describe events.

You might also have an antagonist and other, minor characters. Be careful, though, not to overload your story with characters. You are only writing a few pages and you do not want things to get too complicated.

Top Tip

The protagonist is the main character. Keep your focus on him or her to make the story clear and coherent.

An antagonist is someone opposed to the protagonist or who stands in his or her way.

It is not a matter of 'goodies and baddies' but it does create conflict.

You should also keep your plot fairly simple for the same reason. If you are writing a complete short story, think about story structure and include an inciting incident, a climax and at least one turning point (but not too many). Establish the 'world' of your story but do not spend too much time on exposition. You might end with a shocking or surprising twist – but it should make sense in the context of the story. It has been said that you should give your readers what they want but not in the way they expect. Having planned the story, think about the order you tell it in. There's nothing wrong with simple **chronological order** but you might want to use flashbacks or 'flash forwards'.

If you are writing the opening to a longer story, most of what you write will be exposition so you can take more time over describing characters and settings, but you should be aware of where the story would go if it were complete, so it might be worth sketching out a plan for the whole. It is a good idea to end your piece with the inciting incident. This is the point at which something happens that affects the protagonist and really gets the story going. Stopping at this point should leave your readers wishing that they could read the whole story, and find out what happens.

Descriptive Writing

The descriptive writing task in the exam may give a written prompt, or be linked to a picture stimulus which in itself bears some relationship to the source material used for the writing section. You are not being asked to describe what you see in the picture. This would be rather limiting. The picture is there to stimulate your imagination. It might remind you of a place you have visited or somewhere you have seen on television or read about, or you could use it as the starting point for an imagined world.

Some aspects of descriptive writing to bear in mind:
- Should you use first or third person? Third person is more usual in a descriptive piece and can help to keep the focus on what is being described. If you use the first person, you are putting yourself in it. This can be good especially if you are writing about the memory of a real place. It also allows you to describe feelings. The pitfall is that using the first person can cause you to stray into writing a story.
- Past or present? Either is fine. Present tense can be more vivid and immediate, while past tense can give a sense of reflection – 'emotion recollected in tranquillity'. Just make sure you are consistent (although switching between tenses can be a clever device – as long as it is logical and clearly deliberate).

- Imagery is central to descriptive writing. It could be said to be all about imagery. Think about whether to keep to **literal imagery** or whether to experiment with **figurative imagery** – not just **metaphors** and similes, but **personification** and **pathetic fallacy**. If you do use figurative imagery, avoid clichéd images. Try to surprise the reader with original or unusual comparisons.
- Use all (or almost all) the senses. Avoid doing this in a mechanical way, for example one paragraph for each sense, but be aware that description is not limited to describing what you see.
- In structuring your piece, techniques like 'big to small' (starting with a distant view and closing in on detail) can be useful. This is, however, very common and you might be able to think of something a bit different. Small to big maybe?
- Use descriptive language but don't overdo it. There's a delicate balance here. Some of the best writers avoid adjectives altogether but examiners, looking to see whether your register reflects the purpose of the piece, will probably expect adjectives and adverbs. So use them but try to use them in a relevant and interesting way. A precise or interesting choice of verb can eliminate the need for an adverb, for example 'sprinted' rather than 'ran quickly'.

Top Tip

Be very clear in your mind about whether you are writing narrative or description. You will want to include at least some description in a narrative piece – but don't get carried away and forget your plot. If you are writing a description, be on your guard against it turning into a story.

Technical Accuracy

40% of your marks in the writing section are for the accuracy of your spelling, punctuation and grammar, so do not neglect these.

Punctuation

The most common punctuation error seen in exams is 'comma splicing', which means using commas to join **clauses** without using a connective. In other words, using them when you should be using either full stops or semi-colons. You will see this a lot in print and unfortunately it is getting more and more common, but you should avoid it.

Remember the reasons for using commas and only use them in these ways:

- To separate **subordinate clauses** from main clauses. Subordinate clauses give extra information but are not necessary for the sentence to make sense:

Lucy, having eaten three bananas, felt sick.

Jonathan, who lived next-door, broke our window.

- For separating items in lists:

She bought a coat, three hats, a balloon and an accordion.

- To introduce and end direct speech:

'I've had enough of this,' she moaned.

'Avoid comma splicing at all costs,' warned Mrs Pondicherry.

If you cannot justify using a comma by citing one of these three reasons, don't use it. Find a different punctuation mark.

The mark scheme rewards 'a wide range of punctuation used with a high level of accuracy'. A 'high level of accuracy' means hardly any mistakes. A 'range' of punctuation could include most, if not all, of the following:
- full stops
- commas
- semi-colons – to connect two closely related clauses without a connective or to separate longer items in a list
- colons – to introduce a list, a quotation or an explanation
- question marks – for rhetorical questions and in direct speech
- exclamation marks – use these very sparingly!
- dashes – a less formal, but very useful punctuation mark
- parentheses (brackets)
- inverted commas – for direct speech, quotations or titles.

Grammar

The examiners are looking for a 'full range of appropriate sentence forms' used 'for effect'. You should use a mixture of the following:

- **Simple sentences** – sentences that consist of a subject, a main verb and sometimes an object. An occasional simple sentence can express an important sentiment. A series of them can increase pace and drama.

She shot him.

- Compound sentences – two clauses of equal value joined by 'and', 'or' or 'but'.

I sat on the ground and I wept.

- Complex sentences – sentences containing two or more clauses, one of which could stand as a simple sentence, the others being subordinate. You should use a lot of complex sentences, adding variety by sometimes having the subordinate clause before the main clause and sometimes after it, and occasionally in the middle of it.

As I emerged from my semi-conscious state, I became aware that before me, watching me with a hundred eyes, was a herd of the most extraordinary animals I had ever seen.

- Minor sentences – sentences that are not really sentences because they do not have a main verb. Use them sparingly for dramatic impact.

Never again!

The examiners will also want you to use Standard English consistently and show secure control of complex grammatical structures. This means not only avoiding slang (except as discussed on page 28) but also using correct grammar.

Pronouns

One of the most common mistakes made by students is the misuse of pronouns, especially 'I' and 'me':
- 'I' is the subject and 'me' is the object, so both 'Me and Harry live in Leeds' and 'Harry and me live in Leeds' are wrong. You would not say 'Me live in Leeds'.
- Equally wrong is 'Harry gave a lift to Saskia and I'. You would never say 'Harry gave a lift to I'; you would say 'Harry gave a lift to me'.

If you are not sure about this, take away the extra person and think about whether just 'I' or 'me' is correct.

Agreement and Tenses

In everyday speech people often use non-standard verb forms, for example:
- 'You was really great' instead of 'You were really great'.
- 'She were my best friend in school' rather than 'She was my best friend in school'.

People also often make the mistake of using non-standard forms of the past tense in their writing, for example:
- 'I done my homework' instead of either 'I did my homework' (simple past tense) or 'I have done my homework' (perfect tense).
- 'I give it to the dog yesterday' rather than 'I give it to the dog every day' (present tense) or 'I gave it to the dog' (simple past).

These sorts of usage vary from region to region and might be useful when writing direct speech but they are not Standard English and, therefore, are not usually acceptable in your writing.

> **Top Tip**
>
> Go over work that you have written in the past to see if there are any areas in which you have not been using Standard English grammar. Learn the correct forms and practise using them.

Spelling

Spelling is linked in the mark scheme with the use of 'extensive and ambitious' vocabulary. This is because marks for spelling are not awarded simply on the basis of not making any mistakes. If this were the case, you could get high marks by avoiding using complex or unusual words, but this would not help your writing. The occasional slip-up with a tricky word will not stop you getting high marks. However, you should try to eliminate errors as far as possible. Here are some examples of commonly misspelt words that you would be expected to spell correctly at each level:
- Level 1 (basic) – woman, friend, read, were/where/we're, there/their/they're, too/two/to
- Level 2 (more complex words) – difficult, knowledge, fortunately, interesting, definitely
- Level 3 (complex and irregular) – accommodation, separate, weird, occasional, onomatopoeia, rhetorical
- Level 4 (ambitious vocabulary) – authoritative, proletarian, antimacassar, metaphysical, euphemistically.

Top Tip

Different people find different words difficult to spell. Go back over your school work and pick out words that you have spelt incorrectly. List them and see if you can spot any patterns. Learn the correct spellings.

Question 5

Worked Example

See page 3 for suggestions on how to make effective use of the worked example.

 You have been invited to submit a short story to the school or college magazine. It will be read by people of your own age.

Write a description suggested by the picture.

(24 marks for content and organisation;
16 marks for technical accuracy)   [40 marks]

Sample Answer 1

Stairs. A lot of steep stairs ahead of me.[1] There are handrails on either side and the steps themselves are wide.[2] In addition, they are brightly lit, if anything, the lights are too bright, shining in my eyes.[3] It should not be a scary or a threatening place but I feel trapped because I have no choice. I have to go up the steps. I cannot turn back.[4]

Ahead of me I can see the building. It is niether old nor new. It is built from purple bricks and there must be four or five storys. Each story is defined by a row of cheerful bright windows.[5] Is there anyone in there? I can't see people moving about and it's a bit late for an office building to be busy but the lights are on. Maybe the cleaners are still working. Maybe[6] the lights come on automaticly[7] for security.

At last I am at the top of the steps. In front of me there are plate glass doors, then I see a sign, that says 'Sherman and Jones', it does not say who they are or what they do.[8] There is a low buzzing noise coming from inside the building.[9] Through the doors I seen[10] a wooden desk and a chair. The carpet was blue and worn. The reception desk is wooden and old, there are some dead-looking plants on it. Nobody is there.[11]

It looked desserted but I could hear that noise so someone must be in. There is no door bell. I bang on the door. I can hear steps behind me. There are traffic noises in the distance. My voice echos as I shout 'Let me in!'[12]

[1] Two minor sentences provide a sharp, dramatic opening.
[2] A compound sentence. The description itself is simple but appropriate.
[3] An attempt at a complex sentence, spoilt by comma splicing.
[4] The first paragraph is dramatic and involves the reader but the focus on the narrator and what he/she is doing make it seem more like a story than a descriptive piece.
[5] 'Cheerful…windows' could be seen as personification – a literary device.
[6] **Anaphora** (repetition of 'maybe') – a literary device used appropriately.
[7] This is the third spelling error of a complex but not especially difficult word.
[8] More comma splicing.
[9] The candidate has remembered that there are five senses and mentions a sound.
[10] Incorrect grammar as the writer switches to the past tense for no apparent reason.
[11] Back to the present tense with an effective simple sentence.
[12] More spelling errors in this paragraph. The short sentence adds to tension but the climax is rather clichéd – and again it is looking more like a narrative than a description.

Let's look at it in relation to the mark scheme:

- Content:
  - The register is appropriate to the audience, but not necessarily to the purpose. It keeps straying into narrative and the descriptions are not really developed. There are one or two effective uses of linguistic devices and the vocabulary, while not 'clearly chosen for effect', is reasonably varied. (Upper Level 2)
- Organisation:
  - It is in paragraphs and they are linked by discourse markers such as 'at last'. There are no particularly striking structural features but the ideas are connected and the writing does engage the reader. (Lower Level 3)

For content and organisation this answer just gets into the lower end of Level 3.

Mark **13 / 24 (Lower Level 3)**

- Technical Accuracy:
  - Sentence demarcation is varied. It is sometimes accurate but there is quite a lot of comma splicing. A range of punctuation, though not an extensive one, is used. (Level 2)
  - There is a variety of sentence forms used for effect. There are one or two lapses in the use of Standard English but it is mostly used appropriately. (Level 3)
  - Vocabulary is varied but not sophisticated and there is some accurate spelling of complex words. (Level 2)

This fulfils the demands of Level 2 and, because of the varied sentence structures, just creeps into Level 3.

Mark **9 / 16 (Level 3)**

Total Mark **22 / 40 (Lower Level 3, equivalent to approx. grade 4)**

__# English Language Paper 1

Sample Answer 2

Now let's look at how the answer can be improved.

> *Stairs. A lot of steep stairs ahead.[1] Handrails on either side of the wide steps.[2] The lights are too bright, shining in my eyes.[3] It should not be a threatening place but it feels like a trap about to close. The silence doesn't help.[4]*
>
> *Straight ahead the building rises before me. Neither old nor new, it is built from purple bricks. Some of the mortar between the bricks is crumbling and weeds grow in odd places like tufts of hair on an old man's face.[5] Each of its five storeys is defined by a row of incongruously cheerful bright windows.[6] There is no sign of humanity within. If people still work there, they must have gone home. Maybe the cleaners are still working. Maybe there's a caretaker or security guard somewhere, feet up, enjoying a mug of tea from a flask, watching the football on his television. Or maybe[7] the lights come on automatically at night.*
>
> *If there is a security man, he's probably seen me.[8] There's a CCTV camera winking at me from above the plate-glass doorway. Emblazoned across the glass in fading gold letters are the names 'Sherman and Jones'. It does not say who they are or what they do. A low buzzing noise comes from inside the building.[9] Through the doors I can make out an elderly wooden reception desk and one lonely office chair, foam sprouting from its torn fabric covering. The once patterned carpet is worn; it may have been blue and gold.[10] Nobody is there.[11]*
>
> *That buzzing noise is getting louder – a belligerent wasp about to attack. There is no intercom; there is no bell. The buzz gets louder but still nobody appears in the foyer. I bang on the door. The noise cuts through the silence of the evening gloom. I wait.[12]*

[1] The same sharp, dramatic opening, with two minor sentences.

[2] Another minor sentence.

[3] A complex sentence, this time correctly punctuated.

[4] The first paragraph still has an impact on the reader but the focus is much less on the narrator and more on the surroundings.

[5] A simile – slightly odd but at least not clichéd.

[6] The description of the windows has been improved by the addition of an adverb which would count as 'adventurous vocabulary'.

[7] Anaphora (repetition of 'maybe') – a literary device used appropriately, now developed a little.

[8] Effective integrated discourse marker.

[9] Sound is described for the first time but this time the description of it is developed and a point is made of it being the only sound.

[10] A much more detailed, developed description.

[11] Effective use of a short, simple sentence to end the paragraph.

[12] The ending still seems a little more like a story than a description but this time there has been a lot more developed description and it is less clichéd and obviously dramatic.

Let's look at it in relation to the mark scheme:

- Content:
    - The register is matched to the audience. It is also matched to the purpose now that the description is more developed and the story element has diminished. There are some effective uses of linguistic devices and the vocabulary is much more extensive. (Lower Level 4)
- Organisation:
    - Again, there are no particularly striking structural features but the description develops as the narrator arrives at the building and there is an element of 'big to small'. The writing is engaging and the ideas are more complex. Paragraphs are consistently coherent, with integrated discourse markers. (Lower Level 4)

For content and organisation this answer gets into the lower end of Level 4.

Mark ▷ **21 / 24 (Lower Level 4)**

- Technical Accuracy:
    - Sentence demarcation is consistently secure and accurate. A range of punctuation is used with success. (Level 4)
    - A full range of sentence forms is used for effect. Standard English is used appropriately. (Level 4)
    - Vocabulary is sophisticated and all words, including some ambitious ones, are spelt correctly. (Level 4)

This fulfils the requirements for Level 4.

Mark ▷ **16 / 16 (Level 4)**

Total Mark ▷ **37 / 40 (Level 4, equivalent to approx. grade 8)**

For more on the topics covered in this chapter, see pages 40–43 of the Collins AQA English Language & Literature Revision Guide.

English Language Paper 2
- Writers' Viewpoints and Perspectives: Reading

The Exam

Paper 2 takes 1 hour and 45 minutes. You are advised to spend about 15 minutes reading the source material, which you will be given on a separate insert. This will leave you with 90 minutes, which you should divide equally between answering the reading questions and the writing question.

The source material will be taken from non-fiction sources, such as **biographies**, **autobiographies**, travel writing, newspaper articles or magazine articles. There will be two sources, one written in the 20th or the 21st century and the other written in the 19th century. You will be told where they come from and when they were written. There may be some extra explanation, particularly of the 19th century source, to help you to understand the context.

Skills Assessed in the Reading Section

Just as in Paper 1, this section of the exam assesses skills that you have been acquiring for most of your life: reading, understanding and evaluation. To prepare for the exam, read widely, in as many forms and genres as you can, and think about and discuss what you have read.

To revise for it you need to ensure that you understand what the examiners are asking you to do and practise doing it.

The Assessment Objectives you will be assessed on are:
- AO1 – identify and interpret explicit and implicit information and ideas; select and synthesise evidence from different texts
- AO2 – explain, comment on and analyse how writers use language and structure to achieve effects and influence their readers, using relevant subject terminology to support your views
- AO3 – compare writers' ideas and perspectives, as well as how these are conveyed.

There will be four questions, each addressing a single Assessment Objective.

Read the texts below before considering how to approach each question.

> **Top Tip**
>
> Get into the habit of reading a 'quality' newspaper, such as *The Times, The Telegraph* or *The Guardian* every day. You do not need to read every single article, just those that interest you. Look especially at features and opinion pieces.

Source A – 21st Century Non-fiction

TV PREVIEW
By Will Johnston
The Doctor Who Gave Up Drugs

BBC 1 tonight

In last week's episode TV doctor and infection specialist Dr Chris van Tulleken laid his cards on the table. He thinks we all take too many drugs – not illegal drugs bought from shady characters in dark alleyways, but prescription drugs, routinely dispensed in their millions (a billion prescriptions a year apparently) by GPs in surgeries all over the country.

According to van Tulleken, many of these drugs are not only unnecessary but can be   **5**
harmful. The side effects from everyday drugs we all take, such as codeine and
paracetamol, range from headaches through stomach bleeding to death. Dr Chris
is especially concerned about the overuse of antibiotics, to which we are becoming
increasingly resistant. But just stopping doctors from describing these drugs proved to be no
easy task, as the good doctor learned when he sat in on a GP's surgery. For starters, each   **10**
patient only gets ten minutes. In this time, it's hard to tell the difference between an infection
and a virus. The former requires antibiotics, while the latter will just go of its own accord. In
addition, many patients now ask for antibiotics, which was an eye-opener for me: I thought it
was the doctor's job to prescribe, not the patient's. So, to be on the safe side, avoiding
things getting worse and patients being unhappy, doctors give antibiotics. 97% of patients   **15**
who ask for antibiotics get them. Dr Chris was no different. So not much joy there.

Dr van Tulleken did have some success, though. Wendy, who was taking an eye-watering number of painkillers, was successfully persuaded – by means of a clever ruse on Dr Chris's part – to give up the drugs and exercise instead. She returned to the surgery to announce that she was feeling a lot better. He then took on Sarah, who had been taking drugs for 20 depression for far longer than is safe. His cure for her was somewhat eccentric – cold water swimming – but it seemed to work. I'm delighted Sarah's feeling better but could the NHS really provide a personable young doctor to go swimming in the country with everyone who's diagnosed with depression?

In tonight's episode, as it turns out, Sarah's motivation does drop – the doctor's answer is to 25 provide a swimming coach. Again, fine for her but not really practicable on a large scale. However, tonight we do see a success story that could possibly be replicated in other surgeries. Dr van Tulleken focuses on another group of people who, in his view, are overmedicated: people with conditions such as high blood pressure, high cholesterol and type 2 diabetes. As he points out, these people are not ill. They are given drugs to prevent 30 problems in the future.

A very healthy looking 69-year-old called Mike arrives at the surgery, where he discusses his condition and medicines with the doctor. He has never had a heart attack or stroke and seems to lead a healthy life but tests showed that he had type 2 diabetes and high cholesterol so he is on a cocktail of drugs. One of these is a statin. Statins are among the 35 most commonly prescribed drugs, designed to lower cholesterol, in spite of their many possible harmful side effects. After listening to what Dr Chris has to say about the dangers and risks of taking such drugs, Mike readily agrees to give up his statins. In their place the doctor prescribes a thirty-minute walk five times a week. He persuades several other patients with similar conditions to form a group and walk together, accompanying them on 40 the first one. He also takes a series of tests before and after the treatment. The results – despite a few problems with motivation – are striking, especially with the diabetes patients. This is thought-provoking stuff. Dr van Tulleken's not suggesting we all flush our drugs down the toilet now, but if doctors and patients could just start relying a little less on easy fixes in the form of drugs, we might all be a lot healthier and happier. 45

Source B – 19th Century Non-fiction

This source is an advertising feature in the form of a letter to a newspaper, *The South Wales Daily News*, published on August 26, 1886.

A MOST INTERESTING LETTER. – The following letter will have just now great interest for all our readers: – Dear Friend, – Here I am at last, enjoying my holiday. The severe strain I have undergone for some time past made a complete rest necessary. Acting on your suggestion, I consulted the leading medical man in this place. 'You have been over-working yourself,' said he. 'Many people do – some with the body, some with the brains. The effect is the same.   **5** A woman with the troubles, and cares, and worry of a family, the student preparing for his exam, the merchant at his desk, and the collier working overtime, are all alike overdoing it, and the result is practically the same in each case. Now you want three things – perfect rest, complete change, and a good tonic medicine. Leave your work at home. Lock up your cares and troubles in your cupboard or safe until you return. That is rest. Go to your holiday **10** resort, change air, company, diet, hours, and habits. That is change. Take some good tonic medicine. That will brace up your system. Sea air and bathing will do much, but not all. A sensible use of medicine at the same time will do much more.' I asked him for a prescription. 'Well,' said he, 'I think I cannot do better than tell you to take Gwilym Evans's Quinine Bitters.' I was surprised to hear a medical man recommend a patent medicine. He noted my surprise and **15** smiled. 'Yes,' said he, 'it is strange. But while I know many patent medicines do more harm than good, I have no hesitation in recommending this. It is the best form of tonic medicine I know of. It is perfectly harmless, and taken during a change of air has always proved beneficial.' I paid him his fee, acted on his advice, and every day find myself becoming stronger. I find that most persons here do the same. I can understand now why it is so **20** popular this time of the year, because by using it a person gets twice as much benefit from this change of air. I found some difficulty in getting it here, and so sent my order direct to Mr Gwilym Evans, F.C.S., Llanelly, and by return of post received a bottle. There are two sizes, 2s 9d and 4s 6d.

Question 1

Question 1 addresses the first part of AO1. You are required simply to identify information, which may be explicit or implicit, but which will not be difficult to find. The question will probably give you a list of statements about the contents of Source A and ask you to say whether they are true or not by shading in a box. There are 4 marks available, one for each correct answer. If you shade more than four boxes, only the first four selected will be marked.

Worked Example

See page 3 for suggestions on how to make effective use of the worked examples.

1 Read again the first part of Source A from line 1 to line 22.

Choose four statements below which are true:
- Shade the boxes for the statements that you think are true
- Choose a maximum of four statements.   [4 marks]

A   Dr van Tulleken specialises in infection.   ☐

B   Sarah has been swimming in cold water to help her depression.   ☐

C   After giving up drugs Wendy is in worse pain than ever.   ☐

D   It is hard to tell the difference between a virus and an infection.   ☐

E   The NHS will arrange for a doctor to take you swimming.   ☐

F   Dr van Tulleken believes that most drugs are harmless.   ☐

G   At the clinic GP appointments last about half an hour.   ☐

H   Only 3% of patients who ask for antibiotics are not prescribed them. ☐

The correct answers are A, B, D and H.

Question 2

Question 2 asks you to write about both texts. As with question 1, the mark scheme is based on AO1 only. However, this time you must address both parts of the AO, so that as well as identifying and interpreting information and ideas you must select and synthesise evidence from both texts. The key word here is <u>synthesise</u>, which means bringing together the two texts. The question will ask you to write a <u>summary</u> of differences (or possibly differences and similarities) between the texts. When you summarise something, you put it in a shortened form, selecting the most important points and putting them in your own words. The question will have a focus, for example:

- Write a summary of the differences between the two schools
- Write a summary of the differences between the two writers' views on hunting.

Or (as in the worked example below):

- Write a summary of the differences between the advice and treatment given to the writer of Source B and to Mike in Source A.

Average candidates would be expected to be able to pick out a few differences between the texts, making some inferences and selecting a few appropriate references to the text. A good answer will be more thorough, making 'perceptive' inferences and statements. Essentially this means digging a little below the surface of the text to find the differences, referring to the text to support your points and expressing them in a clear and fluent way.

For example, rather than say…

The first doctor wants Mike to take fewer drugs but the second wants his patient to take them.

…you might write:

The way the two doctors refer to drugs suggests very different attitudes. In Source B the tonic is described as 'harmless' and 'beneficial', whereas the Source A doctor focuses on 'harmful side effects' of Mike's statins.

Both candidates make the same basic point but the second one shows understanding of the texts, showing an understanding of how different attitudes are implied by the use of language, and supporting the point with short, appropriate quotations.

There are pitfalls for able students here. The question is essentially asking you to do something quite straightforward.

Do not:

- compare language, structure and form – that will be covered in the much longer question 4
- give your own opinion – such as 'I think the first doctor is quite right and everyone should be made to do exercise and instead of taking drugs'; you are being asked to summarise someone else's account or views
- write about one text and then the other, or focus on one text at the expense of the other
- compare the audiences and purposes of the texts – again, save this for question 4
- speculate on reasons for or possible consequences of the differences – 'the second doctor is probably just trying to make money out of his patients'.

Do:

- compare the texts as you go along – everything you say about one text should be balanced by something about the other
- write in complete sentences, using connectives such as 'but', 'while', 'whereas', 'however' and 'on the other hand'
- use short quotations, preferably embedded
- show you have inferred from the text by using phrases such as 'this suggests that' and 'implying that'
- keep it short, while making all the relevant points – there are 8 marks so you should spend roughly 8–10 minutes on the question.

Top Tip

But, *while* and *whereas* are conjunctions and are used to join two clauses, making a longer sentence. For example:

- The second doctor prescribes medicine but Dr van Tulleken does not.
- Mike is worried about taking 'a cocktail of drugs', whereas the letter writer is enthusiastic about the 'tonic'.
- While the letter writer is visiting his doctor for the first time, Mike is a regular patient at his surgery.

However and *on the other hand* are adverbials and require a new sentence. For example:

- The 'leading medical man' is happy to prescribe drugs. Dr van Tulleken, on the other hand, is not.
- The 'leading medical man' charges his patient a fee. Dr van Tulleken's treatment, however, is free.

Worked Example

2 You need to refer to Source A and Source B for this question.

Use details from both sources. Write a summary of the differences between the advice and treatment that was given to the patient Mike in Source A and the letter writer of Source B. [8 marks]

This question asks you to summarise differences so you should not mention similarities.

It mentions 'advice' and 'treatment', which covers everything said by the doctors about the patients' conditions and how they go about curing them.

Note that you are asked to compare the experience of the letter writer (the 'I' of Source B) and Mike (mentioned in Source A). You should focus just on Mike and not any of the other patients mentioned in Source A.

The examiners' mark scheme says that to gain full marks (8 / 8 or high Level 4) you need to:
- make perceptive inferences from both texts
- make judicious references / use of textual detail relevant to the focus of the question
- show perceptive differences between texts.

A mid-range answer (4 / 8 or Level 2) would:
- attempt some inferences from one or both texts
- select some appropriate references / textual detail from one or both texts
- show some differences between texts.

Sample Answer 1

Let's look at a middling answer and see how it can be improved.

In Source A Mike went to see Dr Chris off the television who was trying to get people off drugs. The patient in Source B went to 'the leading medical man' when he was on holiday.[1] He was suffering from strain and the doctor said he should have rest and fresh air and take a drug 'Gwilym Evans's Quinine Bitters' which he said was 'perfectly harmless'.[2] This would make him think it was safe to take it.[3] He did this and felt much better. Dr Chris is against drugs and told the other man to stop taking them and go for a walk.[4] He did this and he felt better. I think this shows how much better it is now going to your doctor.[5]

[1] This does show a difference but it is not focused on the question. The candidate tells us something about the doctors, not their advice or treatment.

[2] A reasonable summary of what happens in Source B, supported by appropriate quotation from the text.

[3] A reasonable attempt at inference, though not linked to anything in Source A.

[4] Summarises what happens in Source B but the statement that 'Dr Chris is against drugs' oversimplifies his position and so misrepresents the text. It could be counted as 'an attempt' at inference.

[5] This is not relevant to the question and cannot be inferred from the texts.

The answer does summarise some of the relevant content of the two sources. Quotations from one source are used appropriately. Attempts are made to infer. Differences between the texts are not clear but an awareness of at least one is shown by the references to one doctor prescribing drugs and the other telling the patient to stop taking them.

Mark ▸ **4 / 8 (Level 2, equivalent to approx. grade 4)**

Sample Answer 2

Let's see what the candidate can change and add to lift the answer to Level 4.

> *Mike is 'healthy looking' and comes to the surgery to discuss a range of conditions which have already been diagnosed, whereas the patient in Source B is suffering from 'strain'.[1] The 'leading medical man' of Source B tells the patient he has been 'overworking'. Dr van Tulleken, however, does not diagnose or suggest a cause for his patient's condition.[2] The doctor in Source B tells his patient that he needs fresh air and rest. Van Tulleken suggests 'a thirty-minute walk five times a week', implying fresh air but the opposite of rest.[3] This is to replace statins, one of Mike's drugs, which he agrees to give up. The doctor in Source B, on the other hand, suggests a 'sensible use of medicine', adding a drug while van Tulleken removes one. He says the drug he is prescribing is 'harmless', in contrast with what Dr van Tulleken has to say about the 'dangers and risks' of Mike's drugs.[4] Finally, after the consultation, the Source B patient just goes away and sends for the medicine, implying he has no further contact with the doctor, whereas van Tulleken stays in touch with Mike, organising a walking group and checking on the results.[5]*

[1] A clear difference between the texts, supported by quotation.
[2] Another clear difference, involving some inference and supporting references.
[3] Perceptive inference made; perceptive interpretation of a difference.
[4] Important difference explained; judicious use of textual reference.
[5] Perceptive inference made as another difference is perceived.

This candidate finds five clear and distinct differences between the texts and makes some perceptive inferences. Short quotations are used throughout and are always relevant to the question.

 Top Tip

Try to find at least four points where the texts differ and deal with each one separately.

Mark ▷ **8 / 8 (Level 4, equivalent to approx. grade 8–9)**

Question 3

Like question 2 of Paper 1, this question focuses on language. It will be about one of the sources only. Unlike the Paper 1 question, it does not direct candidates to a specific part of the text. The mark scheme is based on AO2 but is concerned with language and not structure. Just as in the Paper 1 question, you should aim to analyse the effects of the writer's language, support your analysis with well-chosen quotations from the text and use sophisticated subject terminology accurately. See pages 13–15 to remind yourself of what this means in practice.

Worked Example

 You now need to refer only to Source B, the letter to the newspaper.

How does the writer use language to try to persuade the reader to buy Gwilym Evans's Quinine Bitters? [12 marks]

There are no bullet points to tell you what to focus on but it is safe to assume that, as for Paper 1, you should comment on:
• any words and phrases that strike you
• any particular linguistic techniques that are used
• sentence forms.

See page 12 for examples of linguistic techniques and sentence forms that you might want to comment on. As this exam is called 'Writers' viewpoints and perspectives', the writer may well be putting forward an argument and trying to persuade the reader, so might use rhetorical techniques such as **emotive language**, **direct address**, rhetorical questions, repetition and hyperbole. The register might also be adjusted to the intended audience, so you should consider whether it is formal and written in Standard English or informal and **colloquial**. The register might also be influenced by the subject matter, perhaps using specialised terminology, which may or may not be explained depending on the audience. Do not, however, assume that there will be no use of 'literary' techniques such as imagery. You are just as likely to find these in non-fiction as in fiction.

Let's look at a reasonably good answer and see how it can be improved. To achieve Level 3 (roughly equivalent to grade 5) you need to:
• clearly explain the effects of the language
• use a range of relevant quotations
• use subject terminology appropriately.

Sample Answer 1

The writer starts 'Dear Friend' and writes as if he is addressing a friend: 'acting on your suggestion' but then he uses a lot of direct speech to give the doctor's advice.[1] The doctor uses commands, telling him what to do: 'you want three things'. This shows he is in charge and knows what he is talking about.[2]

The language is quite formal. It is all in Standard English and most of the sentences are long, showing that the relationship between the doctor and patient is formal. There are some short sentences like 'That is change' to emphasise points.[3] There are a lot of lists, including lists of three things to show all the ways the medicine can help different people and get the points home to the reader.[4]

Even though he is addressing a 'friend' the writer continues to write formally after finishing the story about the doctor: 'I find that most persons' which might be because people were always more formal then or it might be because he is not really writing to a friend but to a newspaper.[5]

[1] Uses subject terminology accurately ('direct speech') and refers to the text but does not explain the effects of the writer's use of language.

[2] This time the effect of the language is clearly explained. Correct terminology and a supporting quotation are used.

[3] This is a clear, if rather simple, explanation of the writer's use of sentence structures.

[4] An attempt to explain the use of sentence structures / language techniques, though perhaps not as clear as it might be.

[5] An attempt to explain the use of language but it is not really about the effect of the language use – more the reasons for it. An interesting point, though, that might be made in a more relevant way, probably in answer to question 4.

The candidate explains the writer's use of language, sometimes clearly, but does not analyse it. There are plenty of short quotations supporting the points, amounting to 'a range of textual detail'. Subject terminology may not be sophisticated but it is used accurately and clearly: 'direct speech', 'commands', 'Standard English', 'formal'.

Mark ▸ **8 / 12 (Level 3, equivalent to approx. grade 5)**

English Language Paper 2

For a high grade (the top of Level 4), you need to:
- analyse the effects of the writer's choice of language
- select a judicious range of relevant quotations
- use sophisticated subject terminology.

Sample Answer 2

The piece is set out as a letter, with the salutation 'Dear Friend' and the opening 'Here I am at last' suggesting a close relationship with the reader. However, the tone becomes formal. Complex sentences written in Standard English, such as the one beginning 'Acting on your suggestion...' create a serious tone which reflects the subject matter.[1]

The writer reports his consultation, using direct speech, to make the encounter seem more immediate and authentic: these are the actual words of a 'leading medical man'. The formality of his speech gives a sense of his authority, as does his use of imperatives: 'you want three things'.[2] The repeated use of the second person could be addressing not just the writer, but also the readers, who might apply the doctor's advice to their own situation.[3] In a long complex sentence he lists examples of different people who are 'overdoing it', building up a sense of a huge problem which might apply to anyone. Complex sentences are interspersed with simple sentences ('That is change') which give a sense of confidence.[4] Yet, at the same time he keeps his language vague. 'Overdoing it' could mean any number of things as could 'strain'. He does not want to limit his advice to a small number of people by being too precise.[5]

He uses the 'list of three' in 'perfect rest, complete change, and a good tonic medicine', building to the final item, which is the real subject of the text. Later he repeats the phrase 'a good tonic medicine' and at the end of his speech varies this refrain with 'a sensible use of medicine' so that, despite the talk about 'sea air' and 'rest', there is no doubt about what the real cure will be.[6]

At the end of this speech the writer's simple sentence 'I asked him for a prescription' suggests that he is convinced. The next section, in which the doctor recommends 'Gwilym Evans's Quinine Bitters', is stilted in tone as the writer seeks to combine positive language bordering on hyperbole – 'best form' 'perfectly harmless', 'always... beneficial' – with the measured tones of the professional ('while I know') suggesting that the claims made are reasonable *and objective, although the introduction of the product's name has probably alerted readers to the fact that this is an advertisement.*[7]

The writer uses a list of three to describe the aftermath of his visit, building to 'every day find myself becoming stronger'. This might be a convincing climax. However, its impact is lessened by the anticlimactic 'I found some difficulty in getting it here', which might be off-putting until it becomes clear that the statement is leading to a description of how to get the tonic and its price. By now the writer seems to have forgotten that he is supposed to be addressing a friend as he does not sign off. 'There are two sizes, 2s 9d and 4s 6d' gives a rather bathetic, unintentionally comic ending to this story of poor health and miraculous recovery.[8]

[1] A very clear explanation of the effects of language, supported by quotation and using subject terminology accurately.

[2] The candidate is beginning to analyse the language in greater detail. The focus is clearly on the effect on the reader.

[3] Good analysis of the effect of a detail of language, using subject terminology correctly.

[4] More detailed analysis. By now we could say the candidate is using a 'range' of textual reference – and references are well-chosen.

[5] Perceptive analysis of a detail which not many people would have noticed.

[6] More analysis. The use of subject terminology here could be described as 'sophisticated' and the choice of textual reference as 'judicious'.

[7] Good analysis with a very clear focus on the effect on the reader. This student is proving to be very perceptive.

[8] Very sophisticated use of subject terminology applied accurately and perceptively to the analysis. **'Bathos'** (adjective 'bathetic') is defined as 'a lapse into the ridiculous', usually unintentional.

This answer clearly fulfils all the requirements of Level 4. As a whole, it gives a quite sophisticated critical overview of the piece while still analysing the details of language and always focusing on the effect on the reader. It would have easily reached Level 4 without the final paragraph.

Mark   **12 / 12 (Level 4, equivalent to approx. grade 8–9)**

Question 4

The mark scheme for this question is based on AO3:

- AO3 – compare writers' ideas and perspectives, as well as how these are conveyed.

You have already done some comparison of the contents of the texts in question 2 and have analysed the language of one of the texts in question 3. This question is intended to bring together all your reading skills, so you must consider the points below. The examples are about two (imagined) sources on the subject of fox-hunting:

Points to cover	Example
What the different viewpoints or attitudes are	*While Smith is enthusiastic about hunting, Jones considers it 'barbaric in the extreme'.*
Differences between the writers' purposes	*Text B wants to persuade people to support a complete ban on hunting; the writer of Text A seeks to convey his own love of the pursuit in an entertaining way.*
Differences between intended audiences	*Smith does not expect his audience to question the idea of hunting, whereas Jones expects many of her readers to share her passionate anti-hunting views.*
Differences in form	*Jones's article is an opinion piece for a newspaper, essentially a **polemic**...Text A is a personal narrative, taken from an early part of the author's autobiography.*
Differences in tone	*Both writers use some humour, but while Text A is gentle and nostalgic in tone, Text B is sarcastic and quite savage in its attacks.*
Structural differences	*Smith starts his piece with a personal **anecdote** about hunting, which he uses to lead into his argument. Jones's piece is entirely anecdotal, constructed as a story and leading to an exciting climax.*
Differences in the way they use language	*Smith and Jones both write in the first person, but Smith, unlike Jones, addresses the readers directly, using the second person to involve them in the argument.*

Bear in mind that you do not have to cover all the above. There may be, for example, very little you can say about structure. However, a good answer will include most of these aspects. Always try to link 'how' to 'what' by ensuring every mention of the writers' methods is connected to their viewpoints or attitudes. For example:

Not just:

> *Smith and Jones both use a lot of imagery connected to war. Jones talks about 'massacre' and 'wounds'. Smith uses words like 'prize' and 'triumph'.*

Instead:

> *Both writers use the imagery of war. Jones focuses on bloodshed, talking of the 'massacre' of the animals and their 'wounds', which reflects her concern with animal welfare. Smith talks of 'the prize' and 'triumph', glorifying the hunt as others glorify war.*

All your statements should be backed up by quotations from the text.

Top Tip

The texts will convey different attitudes to their subject but they may use similar methods to convey those attitudes. When you compare methods, comment on similarities as well as differences.

Make sure you mention both texts in every paragraph. Do not make a statement about one text without comparing it to the other.

Worked Example

 4 For this question, you need to refer to the whole of Source A and the whole of Source B.

Compare how the two writers convey different attitudes to health and medication. In your answer you could:
- compare the different attitudes that they write about
- compare the methods they use to convey those attitudes
- support your ideas with references to both texts. [16 marks]

This question asks you how the writers convey 'attitudes' rather than 'their attitudes'. This is because in both these texts the writers are reporting the attitudes of others – the 'leading medical man' in the first and Dr Chris van Tulleken in the second. The tone and content of both, however, suggest that the writers share their attitudes.

'Convey' means to put across and the key word 'how' tells you that you should be considering the writers' methods. The exam board sees this question as 'synoptic', which means that it aims to bring together all the reading skills you have developed during the past two years. The mark scheme for AO3 includes elements of AO1, AO2 and AO4. The bullet points given in the question guide you towards looking at these elements. The first is about finding and interpreting ideas and attitudes. The second refers to the writers' use of language and structure to achieve effects and influence readers. The third reminds you to support your ideas with appropriate references.

A reasonably good answer from a student who would expect to gain a Level 3 would:
- compare ideas and perspectives in a clear and relevant way
- explain clearly how writers' methods are used
- select relevant supporting detail from both texts
- show a clear understanding of the different ideas and perspectives in both texts.

The key words here are <u>clear</u> and <u>relevant</u>.

Sample Answer 1

Will Johnston is telling us about a television programme. In the programme a doctor gives his views on how we all take too many drugs and tries to get people to do without their drugs. Source B is a letter to a newspaper about a 'tonic'. The writer wants everyone to take the drug and says they will feel better.[1]

The tone of Source A is quite chatty and uses some humour in phrases like 'shady characters' and 'not much joy'. Source B looks like it is going to be chatty when it starts 'Dear Friend' but the language is formal with a lot of long sentences and phrases like 'I have no hesitation...' from the doctor.[2]

Source B is a personal letter so uses the first person 'I' a lot. It is about a personal experience which is meant to show the drug works. Source A is not personal. It is mostly third person and gives several real examples – Wendy, Sarah and Mike – who have given up drugs and felt better.[3]

Will also uses a lot more medical or scientific language like 'type 2 diabetes' and 'cholesterol', which makes it sound more as if Dr van Tulleken knows what he is talking about, whereas Source B is very vague, just talking about 'strain' and 'overworking'. Maybe this is because modern readers know more about medicine and would understand the terminology.[4]

Finally Source B tells us how to get the drug so we know it is an advert and might not trust what the writer has said whereas Will Johnston is neutral.[5]

[1] A clear comparison of perspectives, including a reference to their different forms.

[2] A good attempt at comparing the writers' use of language, supported by relevant detail, but it is not linked to the effect of the language.

[3] Another clear comparison of the writers' use of language but it is not entirely accurate, not developed and not linked to the effect of the language.

[4] This comparison of the language used does focus on its effect ('makes it sound more as if...') and is clearly relevant.

[5] A clear, if brief, comparison of the writers' perspectives.

This answer does compare perspectives in a clear and relevant way. It does explain some of the writers' methods clearly but does not always make links between methods and effects. Relevant details have been selected from both texts. It shows an understanding of different ideas and perspectives. Generally, it is clear and relevant but a little underdeveloped.

Mark 11 / 16 (Level 3, equivalent to approx. grade 5)

To improve on this mark, the candidate should:
- compare ideas and perspectives in a perceptive way
- analyse how writers' methods are used
- select a range of judicious detail from both texts
- show a detailed understanding of the different ideas and perspectives in both texts.

The key words here are perceptive and detailed.

Sample Answer 2

Source A is a preview of a television programme, the first part of which is more of a review as it covers the contents of the previous episode. In the programme a doctor tries to get people to do without their drugs. Source B is an advertisement for a 'tonic' in the form of a letter to a newspaper. In it a doctor praises the efficacy of the drug and persuades the writer to take it.[1]

Johnston gives examples of people whom Dr van Tulleken has treated without drugs. He seems impressed by the doctor's success but introduces a slightly cynical tone when, referring to Sarah's 'cold water swimming', he asks whether the NHS could really provide a 'personable young doctor' for everyone. Source B is less critical of his doctor but expresses some 'surprise' at the doctor recommending a 'patent medicine' before quickly becoming convinced to use it.[2]

Source A is quite colloquial, engaging the reader with humorous phrases like 'shady characters' and 'not much joy', which lightens its generally serious tone. Source B looks like it is going to be chatty when it starts ('here I am at last') but from then on the language is formal, using Standard English, a mixture of sentence forms and rhetorical devices to convey the doctor's authority ('I have no hesitation') and the power of his argument.[3]

Source B is written in the first person and focuses on the writer's personal experience of the medicine. Source A, on the other hand, is mostly third person as Johnston reports Dr van Tulleken's experience and that of his patients, although the writer does interject his own reaction occasionally: 'thought-provoking stuff'. He is more distant from the subject than the Source B writer, which makes his views more objective.[4]

Johnston uses quite a lot of medical or scientific language like 'type 2 diabetes' and 'cholesterol', which suggests Dr van Tulleken's professional expertise, whereas Source B is very vague, just talking about 'strain' and 'overworking'. This could reflect a lack of precision and medical expertise on the part of 'Mr Gwilym Evans', who makes and sells the drug. There is also a contrast between the individual stories told in Source A about real people who have come off their drugs and the vague generalisations – covering all sections of society from 'a woman with the... worry of a family' to 'the collier working overtime' – of Source B. The former looks like evidence; the latter is merely rhetorical.[5]

Finally, Source B reveals its true nature as an advertisement by telling us how to get the drug. This would lead cynical readers to question all that has gone before, although they may by then have been persuaded to try the 'tonic'. Source A is also trying to persuade the reader – in this case to watch the programme.[6]

[1] Compares ideas and form in a perceptive way.

[2] A very perceptive comparison of the two sources, using supporting quotations from both sources well.

[3] Analyses the writers' use of language and mentions structure.

[4] More analysis of language, well focused on its effect.

[5] Detailed understanding of differences between the two sources' ideas and perspectives, supported by well-chosen quotations.

[6] Perceptive understanding of the different perspectives and the writers' methods.

This candidate has covered a lot of ground in a perceptive, well-written essay, showing understanding of the ideas and attitudes of the two sources. Purpose, audience and form are all commented on, as are tone, language and structure. There is detailed analysis and the points are well supported by a range of references to both texts. It would be difficult to imagine a GCSE student doing much better than this.

Mark ❯ **16 / 16 (Level 4, equivalent to approx. grade 9)**

For more on the topics covered in this chapter, see pages 48–51 of the Collins AQA English Language & Literature Revision Guide.

Skills Assessed in the Writing Section

You will have about 45 minutes to produce a piece of non-fiction writing. There will only be one task. The question will be related in some way to the contents of the sources for the Reading section. It may start with a quotation and ask you to express your point of view on that statement. It will also specify the form in which you are expected to write, and possibly the intended audience, for example an article for a broadsheet newspaper, an article for a website for teenagers, or a letter to a newspaper. As the examiners want to see how well you express your opinions and want you to express them in good Standard English, an article for a broadsheet or a magazine is by far the most likely form.

The Assessment Objectives you will be assessed on are the same as for the Writing section of Paper 1:

- AO5 – communicate clearly, effectively and imaginatively, selecting and adapting tone, style and register for different forms, purposes and audiences. Organise information and ideas, using structural and grammatical features to support coherence and cohesion of texts.
- AO6 – use a range of vocabulary and sentence structures for clarity, purpose and effect, with accurate spelling and punctuation.

The two AOs are assessed separately; AO5 as 'Content and Organisation' and AO6 as 'Technical Accuracy'. The first of these carries 24 marks and the second 16.

Top Tip

Try to finish about five minutes before the end of the exam so that you have time to check the accuracy of your work. If you spot an error in spelling or vocabulary, put a line through it and write the correct word above.

Content and Organisation (AO5)

'Content' refers to whether your writing is suitable for its purpose and audience, and to your use of language.

Your purpose in this paper is to put forward a point of view in a convincing way. You must keep your answer focused on the question, either agreeing or disagreeing with the statement. You may be given a subject about which you feel strongly and/or already have quite a lot of knowledge. This will help. If you do not have a strong view, you can still write a good answer, weighing up the arguments on both sides before arriving at a conclusion. If you feel you know very little about the subject, you may be able to find some useful evidence in the Reading section sources. However, so that all students can have a go, the question will probably be about something most candidates will know about.

Your tone and register should be appropriate to the subject matter as well as the audience. If the audience is not specified, you should write in Standard English for an intelligent adult. Your tone could be serious, light-hearted or a combination of both. Think about these points:

- Whether to address your audience directly, using the second person. Whether this is appropriate depends on the task. In an article for a newspaper you would not normally do this but there are times when it can be effective, especially in rhetorical questions.
- Using a range of **rhetorical devices** – techniques such as rhetorical questions, hyperbole, repetition and lists can be very effective in argument.
- Using humour – you can be witty while putting forward serious arguments.
- Sentence structures – make sure you use a variety of sentence structures and use both **active** and **passive voices**.

> ### Top Tip
>
> The active voice means the subject is performing the action:
>
> *The cat caught the mouse.*
>
> In the passive voice, the subject has the action done to it:
>
> *The mouse was caught by the cat.*
>
> The active voice is often used to make statements seem more objective and, therefore, helps to create a more serious tone.

'Organisation' refers not only to your use of paragraphs but also to how you construct your argument. Here are some pointers that should help you to shape a convincing argument:

- Aim for a powerful opening paragraph, grabbing your reader's attention and making a clear point. You might want to 'deconstruct' the statement, asking what it really means.
- Make sure you have several distinct points to make in support of your argument, starting a new paragraph for each. Five minutes spent planning before you write will tell you if you have enough points. Refer to your plan while writing.
- Structure your argument logically. For example, build up to the most convincing argument, and use discourse markers to link points and 'signpost' the direction of your argument.
- Acknowledge alternative viewpoints but then give your counter-arguments, showing where they are wrong.
- Back up your points with evidence. In the exam you will not have access to actual facts and figures, so it is permissible to make them up.
- Use anecdotes to illustrate your points – but do not depend entirely on them.
- End with a strong conclusion, summing up the main points and stating your considered opinion.

Technical Accuracy (AO6)

For guidance on technical accuracy, see pages 31–34.

Worked Example

See page 3 for suggestions on how to make effective use of the worked example.

'Young people these days are just plain lazy. They sit around playing with computers and eating junk food instead of getting exercise in the fresh air. They're a health disaster waiting to happen.'

Write an article for a broadsheet newspaper in which you explain your point of view on this statement.

(24 marks for content and organisation; 16 marks for technical accuracy)   [40 marks]

Sample Answer 1

This is an outragious generalisation.[1] I know I'm not lazy and neither are most of my friends. I play sport regularly and even made it into the netball team this year. Hurrah! That's not lazy. And I don't often play computer games, I've got a few but I prefer to be running around in the fresh air.[2]

I love Maccies but whats wrong with that? Does'nt everybody?.[3] I don't have them everyday just for treats. And we all like crisps and chocolate. I suppose they are bad for you if you have too many and they lead to diseases like diabetes and bad teeth but I think most of us only have them for treats.[4]

Statistics show that a lot of young people are too fat but it isn't the majority. The majority are quiet healthy and are not obese so they will not be a health disaster. Old people make a lot more problems for the NHS and take up a lot more beds. At least young people have time to change.[5]

And it isn't really there fault. There is so much pressure from adverts and tv to buy unhealthy snacks and drinks. If the government made laws about sugar in food children would not be so unhealthy. And besides, they don't really decide what they eat, there parents do. They need educating too.[6]

And as for computer games, these are not unhealthy, they are good for the brain as they make you think. Playing them dose not mean you can't exercise as well.[7]

Overall, I think most young people are not like the question says but some are and they will have health problems so we should really do something about it and encurrage them to be more healthier like what I am. Get off of your sofas and go outside now![8]

[1] This a strong, striking opening, spoilt by a spelling mistake.

[2] The tone and register do not match the purpose and audience. It is fine to write about yourself but the statement is about young people in general – it is not a personal attack on the writer. There is a variety of sentence structures but there are several punctuation errors.

[3] Rhetorical questions used quite effectively, though 'Maccies' is inappropriate for a broadsheet.

[4] The argument lacks clarity and the tone is probably too informal.

[5] The writer introduces another argument but, again, the message is a bit confused.

[6] Here the argument is developed and more logical.

[7] The writer brings in another argument, addressing part of the statement not yet dealt with. Comma splicing, not for the first time.

[8] Attempts to sum up the arguments and come to a balanced conclusion, but the effect is ruined by poor grammar. The last sentence is not suitable for the form or purpose.

- Content:
  - The candidate attempts at times to match the register to the audience and form, but is too often colloquial. It does suit the purpose most of the time, putting forward lively (if sometimes confused) arguments but the ending belongs more in a promotional leaflet than a broadsheet article. Some linguistic devices, notably rhetorical questions, are used and the vocabulary is reasonably varied. (Lower Level 2)
- Organisation:
  - The answer is in paragraphs and they are linked by simple discourse markers such as 'and as for'. The opening and the ending are quite striking, if not entirely suited to the form. Several arguments are organised in a fairly logical sequence. The style is quite lively and might engage the reader. (Lower Level 3)

Mark 12 / 24 (Upper Level 2)

- Technical Accuracy:
  - Sentence structure is sometimes accurate but there is quite a lot of comma splicing. A range of punctuation is used. (Level 2)
  - There is an attempt to vary sentence forms. There is some use of Standard English. (Level 2)
  - Vocabulary is varied but not sophisticated. There is some accurate spelling of complex words but there are too many spelling mistakes. (Level 2 – just)

  This fulfils the demands of Level 2.

Mark 8 / 16 (Level 2)

Total Mark 20 / 40 (Upper Level 2, equivalent to approx. grade 4)

Sample Answer 2

To say that 'young people…are just plain lazy' is an outrageous generalisation.[1] Of course, there are well documented problems with children's health: childhood obesity is a major concern throughout the world.[2] But it really is not helpful to lump all young people together and suggest that their lifestyles are going to lead to a health Armaggedon. I know I'm not lazy and neither are most of my friends. Contrary to popular belief, while we do enjoy playing computer games, we are not slowly turning into the undead. Most of us occasionally venture out into the fresh air and some of us even take regular exercise.[3]

I am not by any means claiming that there is not a problem, just that we need to get a sense of proportion. For example, so-called 'junk food' is part of 21st century life and hard to avoid. But it is not the work of the devil. Whether it's crisps, burgers or cream cakes, everything's fine in moderation. You won't die from eating a chocolate éclair once a week and a bag of chips on the odd Saturday.[4]

It's a matter of 'moderation in all things', as my Great Grandma (who loved cream cakes, by the way, and lived to ninety-three) used to say. The same old adage also applies to modern technology. The Internet, iPads and mobile phones are all wonderful inventions, which can make our lives easier and more fulfilled, but if we're glued to them (and our sofas) all day and every day, the resultant lack of exercise will be harmful.[5]

Unfortunately, as the worrying statistics about increases in diseases such as diabetes show, not every young person does appreciate the virtues of moderation. There are many possible causes for this: indulgent parents; aggressive advertising; lack of education. The causes are complex but what are the solutions? We can't just sit back and expect the government to sort it out. Slapping taxes on sugary drinks and banning advertisements for junk food are not the answer. If young people are going to change their habits they need to take responsibility for their own health.[6]

The key is education – not just of the children, but of their parents too. Armed with knowledge and understanding, young people can and do make positive choices about their health and well-being. A balanced diet and moderate exercise are all we – adults and children alike – need to keep ourselves fit and prevent that much-prophesied health tsunami from engulfing us.[7]

> *Yes, there is a problem. But generalisation, hyperbole and doom-mongering will not solve it. Much of the evidence does make depressing reading but my own experience tells me that young people can and do take responsibility to improve their own lives. I trust my generation to avert this Armageddon.*[8]

[1] This a strong opening, addressing the question directly and using punctuation accurately.

[2] Tone and register match the purpose and audience. Vocabulary is mature and spelling correct. We already have a range of punctuation.

[3] This use of personal experience is relevant and appropriate, engaging the reader with some self-deprecating humour ('the undead'). 'Armageddon' is ambitious vocabulary. Compound and complex sentences are used in this paragraph.

[4] The argument is starting to develop with the writer starting to express interesting ideas.

[5] The writer moves the argument on, fluently linking this paragraph to the previous one with the reference to cream cakes. An appropriate tone, which is at times personal and quite light-hearted but still addresses the issue seriously, is developing.

[6] The writer acknowledges another side of the argument and answers it. Rhetorical techniques (list of three, rhetorical question) are used as is a range of accurate punctuation.

[7] Arrives at a reasoned, logical viewpoint.

[8] An effective ending, referring to the beginning, focusing on the argument and ending on a positive note.

- Content:
  - The candidate achieves an appropriate tone and register for the purpose, audience and form, engaging the reader with some personal anecdote and wit but remaining focused on the issue. Vocabulary is extensive and ambitious ('Armageddon', 'hyperbole', 'indulgent'). Linguistic devices, including rhetorical techniques and imagery, are well crafted and their use sustained. (Upper Level 4)
- Organisation:
  - Paragraphs are coherent and fluently linked, incorporating a range of ideas. There are no particularly striking structural features but the argument is developed well and the beginning and end are effective. This fulfils the lower end of Level 4 and the fluently linked paragraphs just bring it into the upper end. (Upper Level 4)

  For content and organisation, on balance, this answer is near the top of Level 4.

Mark 22 / 24 (Upper Level 4)

- Technical Accuracy:
  - Sentences are always securely and accurately demarcated. A wide range of punctuation is used correctly. (Level 4)
  - A full range of sentence forms is used for effect. Standard English is used consistently and complex grammatical structures are correct. (Level 4)
  - All spelling of the extensive and ambitious vocabulary is correct. (Level 4)

  This answer fulfils all the demands of Level 4.

Mark 16 / 16 (Level 4)

Total Mark 38 / 40 (Upper Level 4, equivalent to approx. grade 8–9)

For more on the topics covered in this chapter, see pages 52–55 of the Collins AQA English Language & Literature Revision Guide.

English Literature Paper 1

- Shakespeare

The Exam

Paper 1 takes 1 hour and 45 minutes and there are two sections, so you should spend about 50 minutes on Shakespeare (Section A).

There will be six questions, one on each of the six set plays. These are: *Macbeth, Romeo and Juliet, Julius Caesar, The Tempest, Much Ado About Nothing* and *The Merchant of Venice*. As you will have studied only one play, you will have no choice of question. A short extract from the play will be reprinted on the exam paper. The task which follows will probably focus on characters or themes from the play. The bullet points will instruct you to consider the question both in relation to the extract and to the play as a whole.

Skills Assessed in the Shakespeare Section

This section assesses your understanding of, and your ability to analyse, the Shakespeare play that you have studied in class. You should have studied the themes and characters of the play, Shakespeare's use of language, form and structure, and the relationship of the play to its context. There are also a few marks for the technical quality of your writing.

The Assessment Objectives you will be assessed on are:
- AO1 – read, understand and respond to texts. You should maintain a critical style and develop a personal response. You should use references, including quotations, to support your interpretations. (12 marks)
- AO2 – analyse the way the writer uses language, form and structure to create meanings and effects, using relevant subject terminology. (12 marks)
- AO3 – show understanding of the relationship between texts and the contexts in which they were written. (6 marks)
- AO4 – use a range of vocabulary and sentence structure with accurate spelling and punctuation. (4 marks)

Character

There is a very good chance that the question will focus on one of the characters from the play and how he or she changes during the course of the play. It will not simply ask you to discuss the character but will give you an aspect of the character to focus on, for example 'Macbeth as a leader', 'Shylock as an outsider' or 'Prospero as a father'. Alternatively, the focus could be on a relationship, say between Benedick and Beatrice in *Much Ado About Nothing* or Brutus and Cassius in *Julius Caesar*. You might get a question that requires you to look at a group of characters, most probably women (when you should look at a selection of the female characters).

The marks given for AO1 are for your understanding of the meaning of the text and your response to the task, including your use of textual references. You must, therefore, ensure that your answer is always focused on the task, so if the question were about Prospero as a father, for example, you would not spend time discussing Prospero's magic or his qualities as a ruler unless you then related those remarks to his role as a father. For example:

> In all his dealings with Miranda, we are aware that she is not only his daughter but his subject. As a ruler he could be seen as a benign despot; the same applies to his version of parenthood.

The key word in your question will be <u>how</u>, for example:

Write about:
- how Shakespeare presents Prospero as a father in this speech
- how Shakespeare presents Prospero as a father in the whole play.

A variation on this could be 'how far':
- How far do you think Shakespeare presents Prospero as a good father?

This is basically the same but might make you think about what is meant by 'a good father'.

So, how does Shakespeare present characters? In any play you can learn about characters through the following:

- What they say and how they say it
  In **soliloquies** and **asides**, characters speak directly to the audience. You can assume they are telling the truth, revealing their true feelings and intentions. In conversation with other characters, they might lie or 'dissemble', like Lady Macbeth or Don John in *Much Ado About Nothing*.

- What they do
  In *Much Ado About Nothing* Benedick demonstrates his true nature and feelings by agreeing to kill Claudio.
- What other characters say to, or about, them
  Sometimes there is a consensus of opinion among other characters, possibly changing during the play. Macbeth's reputation changes from that of being a loyal and brave soldier to that of a cruel tyrant. A difference in opinion can make us think about both the speaker and the character being spoken about – in *The Tempest* Caliban's relationship with Prospero is very different from Ariel's.
- How other characters react to them
  Julius Caesar's actions and character cause the conspirators to assassinate him but inspire loyalty and devotion in Mark Antony and Calpurnia.

If you consider these four things, taking evidence from the extract and from the rest of the play, you should form a complete picture of how the character is conveyed.

When revising, as a starting point, you could consider the following aspects of each character:

Background	We are told Beatrice in *Much Ado About Nothing* is an orphan who is dependent on her uncle. This influences her actions and those of others.
Personality	We are constantly told that Brutus in *Julius Caesar* is 'an honourable man'. This gains him the respect of others and can be seen in his speech and actions.
Relationships	Juliet's relationship with the nurse is important to the development of the plot.
Motivation	Shylock in *The Merchant of Venice* pursues his 'pound of flesh' because he wants revenge on Antonio (and perhaps all Christians) for the way he has been treated.
Function in the plot	Banquo is with Macbeth when he meets the witches. The prophecy given to him causes Macbeth to murder him, showing his increasing cruelty, and his appearance as a ghost is a turning point in Macbeth's state of mind.

Top Tip

Shakespearean characters are complex and open to interpretation. Different actors – through reading, discussion and rehearsal – can arrive at very different interpretations of the same character.

Draw up a chart listing all the main characters in your play and giving a brief summary of their background, personality, motivation, relationships and function.

Themes

If the question does not focus on a character or characters, it will probably be about one of the play's themes, for example:

- Starting with this extract, explain how Shakespeare presents ideas about love in *Romeo and Juliet.*
- Starting with this speech, explore how ideas about kingship are presented in *Macbeth.*

Even if the question does not focus on themes or ideas, you will need to show your understanding of them, so think about what the main themes of your play are. For example:

- *Romeo and Juliet* – love, families, revenge, fate
- *Macbeth* – kingship, the supernatural, conscience, ambition
- *Julius Caesar* – tyranny, friendship, honour, war
- *The Tempest* – magic, forgiveness and reconciliation, slavery, parents and children
- *The Merchant of Venice* – money, anti-Semitism, justice and mercy, marriage
- *Much Ado About Nothing* – betrayal, friendship, love, appearance and reality.

Most of the themes listed above are present in more than one of the set plays.

Shakespeare, like most playwrights, does not give himself a voice in his plays, so you cannot know precisely what his opinions and ideas were. There have been many different interpretations of his plays over the last four centuries. For example, some critics interpret *The Merchant of Venice* as being anti-Semitic, while others say that in it Shakespeare is exposing anti-Semitism. Some would say that the fate of Romeo and Juliet shows that they should not have defied convention, while others maintain that they are the victims of society. It is not a case of one interpretation being right and another being wrong. Every member of every audience is different and has a different viewpoint. You must come to your own conclusions by looking at the evidence. When thinking about themes you should consider:

- Plot – how themes and ideas are reflected in what happens, for example how Claudio treats Hero when he thinks she has dishonoured him in *Much Ado About Nothing*.
- Images – how Shakespeare presents powerful images to express themes and ideas, for example the opening of the caskets in *The Merchant of Venice*.
- Dialogue – how different points of view are expressed by different characters, for example the discussions between Brutus and Cassius in *Julius Caesar*.
- Soliloquies – how characters 'think out loud' about ideas, themes and issues when addressing the audience, for example Macbeth's speech about the rights and wrongs of killing Duncan.

> ### Top Tip
>
> Acknowledging **ambiguity** and alternative opinions in your answer can only help improve your marks, but you should come to your own conclusion.

Language, Form and Structure

Language, form and structure are not usually mentioned in the question, but your understanding of Shakespeare's use of them accounts for a large proportion of your marks and is essential to answering 'how' Shakespeare does something.

Shakespeare wrote in a mixture of verse and prose. As a general rule, higher status characters speak in verse, while lower status characters, such as servants, and comic characters speak in prose. However, there are exceptions. Most of Benedick and Beatrice's dialogue in *Much Ado About Nothing* is in prose, while Caliban in *The Tempest* uses verse to describe the island. Most of the verse is **blank verse** – unrhymed **iambic pentameter**, the **metre** or rhythm which most closely resembles human speech. It is often said that it also resembles a heartbeat. There are five 'feet' in each line ('penta' means 'five'), each one comprising an unstressed **syllable** followed by a stressed syllable (an **iamb**):

- The <u>quali</u>ty of <u>mercy</u> <u>is</u> not <u>strain'd</u>

The line above from *The Merchant of Venice* follows this pattern. It is regular. In the extract you are given, you might see lines that depart from strict iambic pentameter and so are irregular, perhaps stressing the first syllable of a foot or adding an unstressed syllable:

- I <u>take</u> this <u>offer</u>, <u>then</u>. <u>Pay</u> the bond <u>thrice</u>.

Here the **stress** falls naturally on 'Pay' rather than 'the', interrupting the flow of the line and emphasising the word 'pay'. The presence of **caesura** (a pause in the line indicated by a punctuation mark) immediately before 'Pay' also breaks up the line, conveying Shylock's emotional state.

Occasionally Shakespeare uses different metres, usually for songs or chants, as in *Macbeth* and *The Tempest*.

You should also look out for **rhyme**. Some plays, such as *Romeo and Juliet*, contain a lot of rhyme but in others **rhyming couplets** are used either to end a scene and/or to underline the importance of what is being said.

> If thou read this, Caesar, thou mayst live.
> If not, the fates with traitors do contrive.
>
> *(Julius Caesar)*

Shakespeare uses lots of figurative imagery, including similes, metaphors and personification. Sometimes he uses extended metaphors or **conceits**, where characters develop an idea through imagery. An example of this is when Romeo compares Juliet's hands to a 'holy shrine', extending the idea by comparing his lips to pilgrims, and the idea is then taken up by Juliet. This is one of many examples in *Romeo and Juliet* of characters 'playing with words'. Elsewhere in this play, and others, Shakespeare uses **oxymoron** to express confusion or contradiction, puns and double meanings.

Top Tip
Look for patterns in your play's imagery, for example animal imagery in *The Merchant of Venice* or religious imagery in *Romeo and Juliet*.

Other linguistic techniques you might find include alliteration, **assonance** and onomatopoeia, where the sound of words creates or enhances meaning. Shakespeare often uses forms associated with **rhetoric** (the art of speaking). This is especially true when characters make formal speeches in situations where rhetorical skill would be necessary, for example Mark Antony addressing the crowd in *Julius Caesar* or Portia addressing the court in *The Merchant of Venice*, but he uses them in other situations too. Examples of the kinds of rhetorical devices you might come across in Shakespeare are:

- Rhetorical questions to make the listener think or, as here, to express the speaker's doubts or confusion:

> Wherefore weep I then? *(Romeo and Juliet)*

- Repetition – here used to express Shylock's anger as well as the importance to him of his oath:

> An oath, an oath! I have an oath in heaven. *(The Merchant of Venice)*

- The 'rule of three' – Mark Antony demands the attention of his audience by flattering them, giving them three different titles:

> Friends, Romans, countrymen, lend me your ears. *(Julius Caesar)*

- Hyperbole – here, Cassius exaggerates Caesar's power to persuade Brutus of the danger he poses:

> And this man / Is now become a god *(Julius Caesar)*

Top Tip

It is not enough simply to mention that Shakespeare uses a particular technique or device. You must relate its use to character and themes, and analyse its effect on the audience.

Make sure that you comment on structure in your answer – both the structure of the extract and the structure of the play as a whole. You might consider any changes of subject matter or mood during the extract; if and how the characters or their feelings change during the extract; and anything that breaks up the extract (for example exits and entrances, new speakers). Think about where the extract fits into the play as a whole, ensuring that you remain focused on the task you have been given. If you are writing about a character, look at how that character changes and develops through the course of the play. The extract might come near the beginning of the play before events change the way the character thinks, feels and acts. It could be at a turning point in the character's development, or near the end when the play is about to reach a tragic climax or a happy ending. The second bullet point asks you to write about the whole play. By tracing your character or theme through the play, you are showing an understanding of structure.

Context

The context of a play can include the time when it was written, the place where it was written, where and when it is set, and its literary tradition or genre. It can include consideration of the context in which it is received, which means the different ways in which audiences now and in the past might react to it because of the societies in which they live.

In writing about Shakespeare you need to show an awareness of how the beliefs, assumptions and concerns of his time shaped his plays. You might consider:

Religion	England was a Christian country. Christian beliefs and the Bible are ever-present in Shakespeare but note that there were different denominations and beliefs within Christianity and – as *The Merchant of Venice* shows – an awareness of other religions. Atheism was very rare. Many still believed in witchcraft, astrology and other non-Christian traditions.
Social order	The medieval belief in a 'chain of being' with God at the top was still prevalent as was the idea that everyone had an assigned place in society. King James I firmly believed in the 'divine right of kings', meaning that his authority came from God. However, these ideas of status were becoming less rigid with the growth of the middle classes.
Gender	Women generally were thought to be inferior and subservient to men. Upper-class women had to marry whoever their fathers chose. However, for much of Shakespeare's writing career, England was ruled by a woman, Elizabeth I, and there were many other examples of well-educated or powerful women.
The Classics	Education in Shakespeare's time was based largely on Greek and Roman history and literature. There are many references to classical stories and history.
The theatre	It is worth thinking about how the plays were staged when they were first performed. Most performances were in 'public theatres' like the Globe. The style was not naturalistic and there was little scenery. Performances in private theatres could be more elaborate and plays like *Macbeth* and *The Tempest* were performed with music and visually arresting effects. There were no female actors.

Shakespeare was not always historically or geographically accurate but the times and places where his plays are set should also be taken into account:

- Renaissance Italy, where *Romeo and Juliet* is set, was known both for violent feuds and for being deeply religious. It was also the home of poets who loved experimenting with language and whose work greatly influenced Shakespeare.
- In *Julius Caesar* Shakespeare is faithful to his main source, the Roman writer Plutarch, and the play reflects Roman ideas about honour as well as concerns about replacing the republic with a dictator.
- *The Merchant of Venice* is set in the most successful commercial city of its day. Its characters' concerns with trade and commerce reflect this.
- *Macbeth* is set in 11th century Scotland. There was a real Macbeth. Not much is known about him, but many of the characters existed and quite a few of the events of the play are based on fact.
- *The Tempest* may be set on a magical island but it reflects the Elizabethan and Jacobean interest in exploration and colonisation, especially of the 'New World' of America.
- The Sicily depicted in *Much Ado About Nothing* is probably more like England than Sicily but, as in *Romeo and Juliet*, the themes of disguise, revenge and honour might have seemed rather 'Italian' to Shakespeare's audience.

> **Top Tip**
>
> Do not write separately about context. The examiners do not want a paragraph on the position of women in Elizabethan times. Everything you say should be directly related to the analysis.
>
> Beware of making sweeping generalisations (for example 'Jacobeans thought that…'). Shakespeare's society was very different from ours but – just as in our society – not everybody thought or acted the same way.

Worked Example

See page 3 for suggestions on how to make effective use of the worked example.

Read the following extract from Act 1 Scene 5 of *Romeo and Juliet* and then answer the question that follows.

At this point Romeo has just seen Juliet for the first time.

ROMEO
What lady's that which doth enrich the hand   1
Of yonder knight?

SERVANT
                    I know not, sir.

ROMEO
O, she doth teach the torches to burn bright!
It seems she hangs upon the cheek of night
As a rich jewel in an Ethiop's ear –   5
Beauty too rich for use, for earth too dear!
So shows a snowy dove trooping with crows,
As yonder lady o'er her fellows shows.
The measure done, I'll watch her place of stand,
And touching hers, make blessed my rude hand.   10
Did my heart love till now? Forswear it, sight!
For I ne'er saw true beauty till this night.

Starting with this moment in the play, explore how Shakespeare presents Romeo as a lover.

Write about:
• how Shakespeare presents Romeo in this extract
• how Shakespeare presents Romeo in the play as a whole.   [30 marks]
                                                                AO4 [4 marks]

The focus of the question is Romeo. Clearly, Juliet will also come into your question but only in relation to Romeo. It is about 'Romeo as a lover' so you should not spend time discussing in detail his relationships with his family or friends, unless your comments are related to him as a lover (not as a friend, an enemy, a son, or anything else). The word 'lover' should also alert you to the fact that, although it is primarily about his feelings for Juliet, Romeo's early love for Rosaline should also be mentioned.

Look at the difference between Level 4, 5 and 6 answers:

	AO1	AO2	AO3
Level 6	A critical, exploratory and well-structured argument, supported by a range of well-chosen references. (11–12 marks)	Insightful analysis of language, form and structure, using well-chosen subject terminology. (11–12 marks)	Convincing exploration of one or more ideas/perspectives/contextual factors/interpretations. (6 marks)
Level 5	A thoughtful, detailed and developed response, with integrated references. (9–10 marks)	A detailed examination of the effects of language and/or structure and/or form, using appropriate terminology. (9–10 marks)	Examination of ideas/perspectives/contextual factors possibly including alternative interpretations. (5 marks)
Level 4	A clear, sustained and consistent response, with a range of references. (7–8 marks)	Clear explanation of a range of writer's methods, using appropriate subject terminology. (7–8 marks)	Clear understanding of ideas/perspectives/contextual factors. (4 marks)

The key words for Level 4 (grade 5) are <u>clear</u>, <u>explanation</u> and <u>understanding</u>. To move to Level 5, your answer needs to be more detailed and thoughtful. For the top level (grades 7–9), you still need the detail but you need to explore the text, showing insight, and convincingly arguing a point of view.

Here is an example of a response that should achieve the marks for Level 4:

Sample Answer 1

Romeo has gatecrashed the Capulets' party because Benvolio told him he should forget about Rosaline and look at other girls. He has just seen Juliet dancing and asks a servant who she is but the servant does not know, so he has no idea that she is the daughter of his enemy. He shows here that he is very quick to fall in love. This might surprise the audience as before he was going on about how much he loved Rosaline.[1]

Shakespeare uses a lot of images to express what Romeo feels about Juliet.[2] When he says 'she doth teach the torches to burn bright' he is saying just how much she stands out from the crowd. The simile about 'a rich jewel in an

Ethiop's ear' says the same thing.[3] *He has not spoken to her so he is only talking about her looks: 'beauty too rich for use'. If he can fall in love so easily based on looks people might think he is shallow.*[4] *He calls her a 'snowy dove' because in those days it was good to be very pale.*[5] *He says he will watch her and touch her hand, which will make him 'blessed'. This suggests that he thinks love is holy. If she can make him 'blessed' by touching her she is like a saint.*[6] *Later on he carries on with the idea, calling himself a 'pilgrim'.*[7] *All this suggests his love is true and pure. He asks himself a question, 'Did my heart love till now?' The answer is 'no' so he is saying that he was not in love with Rosaline. Maybe he has found true love or maybe he is just fickle.*

When he speaks to her later in the scene we can see that they have both fallen in love with each other. So unlike Rosaline Juliet feels the same. He goes on using holy images and she does too in a sonnet so we know it is true love.[8] *He is very intense as a lover and enthusiastic so he climbs over the wall to see her on her balcony. In that scene he pledges his love and she makes him prove he is honourable by agreeing to marry her. His love is so strong that he is willing to defy his parents. He will not fight Tybalt at first because he is Juliet's cousin but then he kills him, which means he has to leave Verona. He is so much in love that he cannot bare to be away and threatens to kill himself but is persuaded by the Friar not to.*[9] *Finally, thinking she is dead, he does kill himself. This shows how much he loves her. In the end he is a tragic lover because the strength of his love for Juliet brings about their death, but it does some good when the families are reconciled.*[10]

[1] Clear, explained focus on the task (AO1).

[2] Comment on writer's method and use of correct terminology (AO2).

[3] Clear explanation of the writer's methods – relevant terminology (AO2).

[4] Explanation focused on task, supported by relevant quotation (AO1/AO2).

[5] Some understanding of context (AO3).

[6] Explained response supported by references. This explanation is getting more detailed (AO1).

[7] Clear reference to another part of the text (AO1).

[8] More references to the rest of the text, here explaining the writer's methods, using relevant terminology (AO1/AO2).

[9] Shows understanding of the whole text. Tends to re-tell the story but keeps focus on Romeo as a lover. Lacking in references to the text (AO1).

[10] Focuses on the task (AO1).

- AO1: The response is clear and sustained, though perhaps not consistent as it strays into story-telling. There is a range of references, at least in the first part. (7 / 12, Lower Level 4)
- AO2: There is a clear explanation of the writer's methods, including comments on language and structure. Level 4 – not quite detailed enough for Level 5. Appropriate terminology is used. (8 / 12)
- AO3: Context is considered briefly and ideas about love discussed – not quite enough for Level 4. (3 / 6)
- AO4: 3 / 4

Mark ▶ **21 / 34 (Level 4, equivalent to approx. grade 5)**

To move this answer into Level 5 the candidate needs more detail, more analysis, more extensive and integrated use of quotation, and more discussion of context and alternative interpretations. It is more difficult to describe exactly what is needed to go up another level, as examiners' instructions on the top grades often seem a little vague. They use words like 'conceptualise' and 'overview', which can leave students and teachers in the dark. Make sure you keep a tight focus on the question and that you are putting across your own viewpoint, rooted firmly in the text.

Sample Answer 2

This is a crucial point in the play, the first meeting of Romeo and Juliet. From his opening question to the servant ('What lady's that...') it is clear that Romeo has fallen in love with Juliet. When the servant replies 'I know not' the audience, already aware that Juliet is the daughter of his enemy, is alerted to the possible tragic outcome of this love.[1]

The following speech can be seen as a soliloquy, addressed to the audience and therefore expressing his true feelings, in contrast with his speeches about his love for Rosaline, which were addressed to Benvolio.[2] A series of images emphasise how Juliet is superior to other women. 'She doth teach the torches to burn bright' is an arresting visual image, especially as the stage may well be lit by torches. 'A rich jewel in an Ethiop's ear', like 'enrich the hand' compares her to something precious and continues the idea of her as a bright light in the darkness. The contrast between light and dark – a recurring motif in the play – is continued with 'a snowy dove trooping with crows'.[3] This simile might have resonated more with an Elizabethan than a modern audience, as pale skin was considered desirable. Juliet is protected from the sun and from society. Her fair skin shows both that she is rich and that she is innocent.⁴ Doves also have connotations of purity. At this point he has not spoken to her so everything he says is about her looks, her 'beauty too rich for use'. It would be reasonable, therefore, given that not long ago he was telling Benvolio that 'thou canst not teach me to forget' Rosaline, to infer that he is fickle and his ideas about love shallow. He may come across as sincere and passionate but is he just moving from one unrequited infatuation to another?⁵

The last four lines of the speech signify a change as he moves to a plan of action.⁶ He intends to touch her hand, which will make him 'blessed', implying she is like a saint. Later on, he extends the metaphor calling his lips 'pilgrims'.⁷ This use of religious imagery might suggest that his love is holy. On the other hand, it could be seen as dangerously blasphemous, creating a false idol out of Juliet.⁸ Finally, he asks the rhetorical question, 'Did my heart love till now?'. The answer 'I never saw true beauty till this night' puts his love for Rosaline firmly in the past – though it might be noted that he is still concerned primarily with the 'beauty' of the loved one.

As the scene develops, audiences may become convinced that his love for Juliet is different from his 'old desire'. The mutuality of their love is stressed by their declaration of love in the form of a shared sonnet. Before he talked about love itself, not the loved one, in oxymorons such as 'father of lead' and 'cold fire', suggesting confusion as well as self-indulgence.⁹ He now focuses on Juliet, using hyperbolic imagery to express his intense love. This continues in the 'balcony scene'. Here he is an ardent lover, seeking 'satisfaction', we assume sexual satisfaction, from Juliet. But he also pledges his love honourably, agreeing to marriage.¹⁰ His sincerity cannot now be doubted yet the strength of his love is dangerous and the association of love with death is ever-present. We know that his death is inevitable from the prologue and, as Friar Lawrence warns, 'these violent delights have violent ends'.¹¹ Finally, thinking Juliet is dead, he kills himself. This shows the intensity of his feelings as a lover, but it also shows that he is impetuous – if he had waited he would have known she was alive – and that he cannot see beyond his emotions. In the end he is a tragic lover because his love for Juliet leads to both their deaths, but we might also feel that the 'story of… woe' has been brought about by a lover whose emotions, though deep and sincere, are too extreme and lead unnecessarily to 'violent ends'.¹²

1 Clearly explained, focused response to the task (AO1) with clear explanation of the use of structure (AO2).

2 Clear explanation of use of techniques, related to task and whole text (AO1/AO2).

3 Detailed examination of the effects of language, well supported by reference to the text and related to the whole play (AO2).

4 Thoughtful examination of ideas related to context (AO3).

5 Examination of alternative interpretations (AO3). The response is becoming critical and exploratory (AO1).

6 Moves to a consideration of the whole text with a reference to structure (AO2).

7 Detailed examination of language, well supported by quotations (AO2).

8 Insightful analysis of language (AO2) and convincing exploration of ideas/contextual factors (AO3).

9 Insightful analysis of form and structure, supported by well-chosen subject terminology (AO2).

10 This has developed into a critical, exploratory and well-structured argument (AO1).

11 Thoughtful consideration of ideas, focused on the task, supported by a well-chosen reference (AO1/AO2).

12 The last sentences summarise the candidate's response, clearly focusing on the task (AO1).

- AO1: Critical, exploratory and well-structured approach to task and whole text. Well-chosen references. 12 / 12 (Level 6)
- AO2: Analysis of language, form and structure, using well-chosen and accurate terminology, exploring the effects of the writer's techniques on the audience. 12 / 12 (Level 6)
- AO3: Convincing exploration of different ideas and perspectives, linked to context. 6 / 6 (Level 6)
- AO4: 4 / 4

Mark ▸ **34 / 34 (Level 6, equivalent to approx. grade 9)**

 For more on the topics covered in this chapter, see pages 60–67 of the Collins AQA English Language & Literature Revision Guide.

The Exam

Paper 1 takes 1 hour and 45 minutes and there are two sections, so you should spend about 50 minutes on The 19th Century Novel (Section B).

There will be a question on each of the seven set books:
- *The Strange Case of Dr Jekyll and Mr Hyde* by Robert Louis Stevenson
- *A Christmas Carol* by Charles Dickens
- *Pride and Prejudice* by Jane Austen
- *Great Expectations* by Charles Dickens
- *Frankenstein* by Mary Shelley
- *The Sign of Four* by Arthur Conan Doyle
- *Jane Eyre* by Charlotte Brontë

As you will have studied only one novel, you will have no choice of question. The style of the question is the same as for Shakespeare. A short extract from the novel will be reprinted on the exam paper. This will be followed by the question and two bullet points instructing you to consider the question both in relation to the extract and to the novel as a whole.

Skills Assessed in The 19th Century Novel Section

This section assesses your understanding of, and your ability to analyse, the novel that you have studied in class. You should have studied the themes and characters of the novel, the writer's use of language, form and structure, and the relationship of the novel to its context.

You will be assessed on the same Assessment Objectives and against the same mark scheme as for Shakespeare, except that there is no mark for AO4.

See page 68 for details of AO1, AO2 and AO3.

Character and Narrative Voice

There is a very good chance that the question will be about a character – or characters – from your novel. As with Shakespeare, when writing about characters you should consider:

- what they say and how they say it – Scrooge in *A Christmas Carol* leaves us in no doubt about his feelings about Christmas
- what other characters say to and about them – Utterson and other characters in *The Strange Case of Dr Jekyll and Mr Hyde* discuss both Hyde and Jekyll as they try to understand what is going on
- how they act and react – in *Pride and Prejudice*, Darcy's actions on finding Lydia and Wickham reveal his true character.

When studying a novel there is one more, very important, thing to take into account:

- what the writer/narrator says about characters.

The narrator of a novel will often comment directly on characters, describing their backgrounds, appearance and personalities. Whether these comments are to be taken at face value (as a reliable assessment of the characters) depends on the narrative style of the novel.

When studying any novel, you should think about the narrative voice. Is it mainly written in the first or the third person? *The Sign of Four*, *Frankenstein*, *Great Expectations* and *Jane Eyre* are first person narratives, while *The Strange Case of Dr Jekyll and Mr Hyde*, *Pride and Prejudice* and *A Christmas Carol* are third person narratives. You should also consider how the narrative is structured.

The Sign of Four

The narrator of *The Sign of Four* is Dr Watson. Conan Doyle's choice of Watson as narrator allows the reader to become closely involved with the story of how Holmes solves the case without being privy to his thought processes. Instead, we know only what Watson knows. He is set up as a reliable narrator – a doctor who is objective and intelligent – but he is always a step or two behind Holmes. In this way tension and mystery are created. Watson is an engaging personality and his relationship with Holmes – admiring, critical and sometimes irritated – is important, but he is not at the centre of the novel. He acts as a bridge between the action and the reader. Towards the end of the novel there is another narrator – Jonathan Small – whose narrative explains the mystery.

Frankenstein

Frankenstein also has more than one narrator. In this case, there are several layers of narrative, a technique not unusual in the **Gothic** tradition that helps to give the story the feeling of a **myth** or legend. First, there are Walton's letters to his sister. Within them is Frankenstein's own story and, within that, the story told to him by the creature. Walton is a dispassionate observer, there to lead us to Frankenstein, who to some extent interprets the story for the reader. Walton is a reliable narrator. Frankenstein is the protagonist as well as the narrator. The reader shares his thoughts and feelings and may empathise with him. The creature's narrative serves both to fill in gaps in the story and to shift the reader's sympathies to him.

Great Expectations and Jane Eyre

Great Expectations and *Jane Eyre* are both written as if they were the narrators' autobiographies, tracing their development from childhood into adulthood. This sort of novel is often called by the German name **Bildungsroman**. In both cases the **eponymous** characters write as if they were looking back on their lives. Both tell their stories in chronological order and both reflect on the thoughts and feelings of their younger selves, occasionally addressing the reader directly. They do not, however, 'give away' how things turn out for them until they reach the end. Pip in *Great Expectations* is a **naïve narrator** (one who is innocent and perhaps too trusting of others) and his naïvety might at times lead to his narration being unreliable as he misunderstands people and situations. Jane Eyre, too, can be naïve but she is conscious of telling her story clearly and accurately, even if she does not always know the full story.

The Strange Case of Dr Jekyll and Mr Hyde

The Strange Case of Dr Jekyll and Mr Hyde is a third person narrative that contains first person narratives. The 'framing' narrative centres on Mr Utterson and we see the story unfolding as he does but he is an observer, not the protagonist of the story, and remains a neutral – rather detached – observer, whose thoughts and feelings are not probed. The reader gradually learns the truth about Hyde as Utterson does, through the narrative of Dr Lanyon and finally through Jekyll's own first person narrative.

A Christmas Carol

The narrator of *A Christmas Carol* is an omniscient, or all-knowing, narrator. He knows everything that goes on and sees into everyone's thoughts. Although this is a third person narrator, the story-teller does not remain detached. From time to time he addresses the reader directly, commenting on the characters (particularly Scrooge) and the action, so can be described as an **intrusive narrator**. His style can be informal, even chatty, as if he is telling the story personally to the reader. We feel as if Charles Dickens is talking to us.

Pride and Prejudice

Jane Austen is not as much of a presence in *Pride and Prejudice*, although she does make comments, often sharply ironic ones, on her characters. She also chooses not to be omniscient, keeping information from the reader and allowing us to share Elizabeth's misconceptions. She does, however, share Elizabeth's thoughts and feelings. This type of narration is sometimes known as '**free indirect discourse**'. Austen also allows us access to the thoughts of others, and to events in which Elizabeth does not partake, by means of letters. Letters were a common structural device at the time. Many popular 18th century novels consisted entirely of letters between characters.

> **Top Tip**
>
> An omniscient narrator is one who knows everything, seeing into the thoughts and feelings of all the characters.
>
> An intrusive narrator is one who interrupts the story to speak directly to the reader.
>
> An **unreliable narrator** is one whose version of events cannot be trusted.

Themes

If the question does not focus on a character, or perhaps the relationship between characters, it will probably focus on one of the novel's themes, for example:

*   Starting with this extract, write about how Austen presents ideas about love and marriage in *Pride and Prejudice.*
*   Starting with this speech, how does Dickens present ideas about the spirit of Christmas in *A Christmas Carol*?

Even if the question focuses on characters rather than themes or ideas, you will need to show your understanding of them, so think about what are the main themes of your novel. For example:

- *The Strange Case of Dr Jekyll and Mr Hyde* – the nature of evil, the uses of science, fear.
- *A Christmas Carol* – the spirit of Christmas, the condition of the poor, money and power.
- *Great Expectations* – growing up, friendship, money.
- *Jane Eyre* – the position of women, the power of love, truth and lies.
- *Pride and Prejudice* – marriage, social class and snobbery, families.
- *Frankenstein* – 'playing God', nature and nurture, pride and ambition.
- *The Sign of Four* – finding the truth, greed, murder.

Some of the themes listed above were of interest to many 19th century writers and are present in more than one of the set novels. They are explored through the following:

Plot and events	At the end of *The Sign of Four,* when the box is opened, Watson realises the futility of pursuing wealth. Frankenstein's actions make us think about the ethics of science.
The narrative	Throughout *Jane Eyre* Jane asserts her independence and her moral principles. Jane Austen opens *Pride and Prejudice* with a witty comment on the marriage market.
Characters	Dr Jekyll and Mr Hyde are two sides of the same person, making us think about the nature of good and evil. The Cratchits show Scrooge the true meaning of Christmas in *A Christmas Carol*.
Settings	In *Frankenstein* the mountains are a source of healing, while the icy wastes reflect Frankenstein's despair. Satis House in *Great Expectations* is joyless and barren.
Symbols and motifs	In *A Christmas Carol* the children – Ignorance and Want – represent what Dickens sees as the evils of society. Fire, symbolising passion, is a recurring motif in *Jane Eyre*.

 Top Tip

When you are revising, pick out and learn a few short (just two or three words) and memorable quotations for each important character.

Language

All the novels are written in Standard English. However, there are differences in tone and style. You will be asked to closely analyse an extract from your novel so you should look for use of language that is typical of the novel and for anything unusual or striking. As well as considering the narrative voice (see page 84), you could comment on the language used to describe people and places, and the sort of language used by different characters and what it tells you about them.

Dickens's language is often descriptive and sometimes extravagant, with long sentences made up of lists and/or subordinate clauses as he piles detail upon detail. You might find examples of techniques such as metaphors, similes, alliteration and assonance. Charlotte Brontë uses both literal and figurative imagery to create atmosphere; her descriptions – such as that of the tree struck by lightning – are often symbolic. Mary Shelley's descriptions of the natural world can also be symbolic. Conan Doyle and Stevenson, like Shelley, often use scientific language as befits their subject matter.

Characters often have quirks of speech, even catchphrases like Scrooge's 'humbug' in *A Christmas Carol*, Wemmick's 'the aged P' in *Great Expectations* or Mr Collins's constant dropping of Lady Catherine de Burgh's name in *Pride and Prejudice*. In *Jane Eyre* Rochester's social position and his forceful nature are reflected in his use of imperatives. In *Great Expectations* Magwitch's pronunciation is shown phonetically, for example 'wittles'. This shows the difference in social class between him and Pip, while his cursing adds to the shock of his sudden appearance. Joe Gargery's social class and regional background are also shown in his speech.

Form and Structure

You will need to comment on structure to gain high marks. First, consider which part of the novel the extract has been taken from. If it is from near the beginning, think about exposition: how is the writer introducing characters, themes and settings? *Pride and Prejudice* opens with a generalisation about marriage, followed by dialogue that introduces us to the Bennet family. In *Great Expectations* Pip introduces himself to the reader in an amusing way before suddenly changing the mood with the shocking appearance of Magwitch. If the extract is from near the end of the novel, think about how the writer has resolved the plot and what sort of mood we are left with. In *Jane Eyre* and *Pride and Prejudice*, the protagonists have overcome obstacles to achieve a happy ending in marriage. The mystery of *The Sign of Four* is solved to everyone's satisfaction. *The Strange Case of Dr Jekyll and Mr Hyde* and *Frankenstein* leave us with tragic and sombre endings to reflect on. If the extract is from another part of the book, it may well represent a turning point in the plot. Think about what has gone before and what will come later. Does something happen in this passage that changes the character and/or the story?

All the set texts tell their stories mostly in chronological order. However, many of them contain sections where part of the story is told in 'flashback', often by a different narrator, sometimes in a long speech, sometimes in a letter. Consider whether the extract comes from such a section and how and why it differs from the rest of the narrative.

Look also at the form and structure of the extract itself. You might be able to trace changes of setting, subject or mood between the paragraphs. You might be able to comment on the use of direct speech or of structural features such as repetition, varied sentence structure or paragraph length.

Top Tip

When revising, make a brief chapter-by-chapter summary of your novel to help you understand the overall structure.

Context

The examiners have made it clear that 'context' includes not only the time and place in which the text was written but also the literary tradition to which it belongs.

It is easy to make generalisations about life in the 19th century, for example 'Women had no power' or 'Everybody went to church', but the more you study the period the more you will realise that it was a time of great change and diversity of thought. The novels reflect that.

19th Century Concerns

Interest in scientific and psychological research, its impact on society and the moral questions arising from it are reflected in *Frankenstein* and *The Strange Case of Dr Jekyll and Mr Hyde*. Dickens wrote *A Christmas Carol* to make his readers think about the plight of the poor and the inequality of Victorian society. Jane Austen and Charlotte Brontë were both concerned in their novels about women's lack of independence and power, but they were not campaigning feminists and they did not reject conventional ideas altogether.

What all the novels have in common is a concern with morality. Characters in 19th century novels are faced with difficult circumstances and make moral choices. Sometimes they make bad choices and suffer the consequences. Sometimes the right choice is that dictated by conventional morality and religion; sometimes it is at odds with the society they live in.

Genre and Literary Context

It is important to think about – and in the exam to show that you have thought about – genre and literary tradition. Novels became hugely popular in the 19th century as more and more people became literate. Many went to lending libraries or bought magazines, such as Dickens's *Household Words* in which he and other novelists published their latest books in serial form. Novels could tackle serious issues in an accessible way or simply provide entertainment.

Jane Austen wrote at the end of the 18th, and early 19th, century and her work reflects the rational ideas of the 18th century 'Augustans'. Like many of them she uses **satire** to criticise people and society in a comic way. However, she wrote at the time of the Romantic poets, who valued emotion over reason. In her work we can almost see a debate between these traditions and she seems to promote a compromise of moderation and balance.

A few years later, Mary Shelley fully embraced the Romantic tradition in *Frankenstein*. However, *Frankenstein* is more often described as Gothic than Romantic. This genre is related to **Romanticism** but is more sensational, using horror and the supernatural to thrill and entertain its readers. *Jane Eyre*, *Great Expectations*, *A Christmas Carol* and *The Strange Case of Dr Jekyll and Mr Hyde* all contain Gothic elements. In the first two there are moments when the writers use heightened language and a sense of mystery to disturb the reader and create tension, for example the fire in *Jane Eyre* and the appearance of Magwitch in *Great Expectations*, but overall they are serious works concerned with the psychological development of their protagonists and their place in society.

In *A Christmas Carol*, Dickens consciously uses a popular form of Gothic, the ghost story, to get across a serious message. Stevenson uses a horror story to explore ideas of good and evil. Both writers knew that the supernatural element of their novels would sell copies. *The Strange Case of Dr Jekyll and Mr Hyde* also contains elements of the newly popular detective story, a genre developed and popularised by Conan Doyle in his Sherlock Holmes stories.

> **Top Tip**
>
> Remember that 'context' is not just about history but also about literary traditions. Any discussion of social, historical or literary context should be related directly to the novel.

Worked Example

See page 3 for suggestions on how to make effective use of the worked example.

Jane Eyre by Charlotte Brontë

Read this extract from chapter 2 and answer the question that follows.

Jane has been left alone in the red-room as punishment for her behaviour.

This room was chill, because it seldom had a fire; it was silent, because remote from the nursery and kitchen; solemn, because it was known to be so seldom entered. The housemaid alone came here on Saturdays, to wipe from the mirrors and the furniture a week's quiet dust; and Mrs Reed herself, at far intervals, visited it to review the contents of a certain secret drawer in the wardrobe, where were stored divers parchments, her jewel-casket, 5 and a miniature of her deceased husband; and in those last words lies the secret of the red-room – the spell which kept it so lonely in spite of its grandeur.

Mr Reed had been dead nine years: it was in this chamber he breathed his last; here he lay in state; hence his coffin was borne by the undertaker's men; and, since that day, a sense of dreary consecration had guarded it from frequent intrusion. 10

My seat, to which Bessie and the bitter Miss Abbot had left me riveted, was a low ottoman near the chimney-piece; the bed rose before me; to my right hand there was the high, dark wardrobe, with subdued, broken reflections varying the gloss of its panels; to my left were the muffled windows; a great looking-glass between them repeated the vacant majesty of the bed and the room. I was not quite sure whether they had locked the door; and 15 when I dared move, I got up and went to see. Alas! yes: no jail was ever more secure. Returning, I had to cross before the looking-glass; my fascinated glance involuntarily explored the depth it revealed. All looked colder and darker in that visionary hollow than in reality: and the strange little figure there gazing at me, with a white face and arms specking the gloom, and glittering eyes of fear moving where all else was still, had the 20 effect of a real spirit; I thought it like one of the tiny phantoms, half fairy, half imp, Bessie's evening stories represented as coming out of lone, ferny dells in moors, and appearing before the eyes of belated travellers. I returned to my stool.

English Literature Paper 1

Starting with this extract, how far do you think Brontë presents Jane Eyre as an outsider?

Write about:
- how she presents Jane in this extract
- how she presents Jane in the novel as a whole.   [30 marks]

The extract is taken from near the beginning of the novel, so Brontë is at this point clearly establishing Jane's character and situation.

The question about being an 'outsider' is a popular one with examiners in the Shakespeare, 19th Century and Modern sections of the exam. Perhaps this is because so many protagonists in literature are seen or see themselves as 'different' and at odds with society. Questions like this make it comparatively easy to discuss context.

The phrase 'how far do you think' suggests that you may feel that Jane Eyre is only an 'outsider' to a certain extent or perhaps not at all. You will need to consider in what ways she is an outsider and in what ways she is not.

The bullet points remind you to analyse the passage closely and then to write about the whole novel. Given that this is quite a long novel, you will have to think about which parts of it you should focus on.

Below is an answer which should achieve Level 4 (about grade 5). To remind yourself of the requirements of Levels 4, 5 and 6, refer to page 78.

Sample Answer 1

Brontë starts by describing the room. She uses three adjectives, 'chill', 'silent' and 'solemn' and explains each one. The first two are literal because it is a cold and quiet room but the third 'solemn' makes it sound depressing.[1] There is a 'week's quiet dust' which shows the room is not used and has no life in it. So far it is not frightening but in the last sentence of the first paragraph Brontë mentions the 'secret' that makes it 'lonely'.[2] The short second paragraph tells us it is where someone died and where he lay in his coffin. Jane is very young and to put her in a room that is isolated shows that she does not belong to the family.[3] Mrs Reed wants to punish her and has blamed her instead of her own son, making her feel not part of the family.

In the third paragraph she describes the room in detail from a child's point of view. Its 'vacant majesty' shows how isolated and unloved it is – like Jane herself. It is also like a 'jail'. Jane looks at herself in the mirror and describes what she sees – a 'strange little figure'.[4] This shows that she sees herself even at this age as odd and different. She calls herself 'it' as if even she does not have feelings for herself and describes herself as 'half imp, half fairy', as if she does not belong in the normal world.[5]

Throughout the novel she refers to herself as odd, small and not good looking.[6] This seems important to her and she thinks she is being judged by her looks. She is also an outsider because she is an orphan. Mrs Reed is cold to her and then she is sent away to school.[7] But she settles in at school and seems to belong there. Only when she leaves she has to become a governess so at Thornfield she is neither one thing nor the other. She does not belong with the guests or with the servants.[8] She sits watching the party but not joining in. On the other hand, Rochester does try to include her and when she finds the Rivers family she is welcomed. If she was an outsider before she is not now.[9] When she returns to Rochester she definitely is no longer an outsider. She now has money of her own as well as a rich husband. She might be a bit 'odd' and different and not always wanted but she does not remain an 'outsider'.[10]

[1] Clear explanation of writer's methods, supported by quotation and using some subject terminology (AO2).

[2] Understanding of structure shown. The candidate has not yet focused on the question about being an outsider (AO2).

[3] Focus on the question – clear explanation of how she is an outsider (AO1).

[4] Focuses much more on the question with good use of quotation and explanation of the effects of language (AO1/AO2).

[5] Explanation of writer's methods, focused on question. The candidate is beginning to analyse, which could bring the answer into Level 5 (AO1/AO2).

[6] The candidate moves to a consideration of the whole text (AO1).

[7] Clear explanation of how and why she is an outsider (AO1).

[8] Understanding of context (her position as a governess) (AO3).

[9] The candidate is addressing the question clearly, weighing up 'how far' she can be seen as an outsider, referring to incidents in the novel (AO1).

[10] This sums up the candidate's opinion, answering the question clearly and showing some understanding of the novel's structure. Some understanding of contextual factors shown (AO1/AO2/AO3).

- AO1: The response is clear and sustained. Although it takes a while to start answering the question, when the candidate does there is a clear engagement with the question of 'how far'. There is a range of reference – good use of quotations in the first part and some clear references to other parts of the text. 8 / 12 (Level 4)
- AO2: Clear explanation of the writer's methods, including many comments on language and some on structure. At times there is detailed analysis, which could be considered Level 5. 8 / 12 (Level 4)
- AO3: Context is considered in the comments about Jane's position as a governess. An understanding of contextual factors is implied but ideas about being an outsider in the society of the novel are not developed and literary traditions are not mentioned at all. 4 / 6 (Level 4)

Mark **20 / 30 (Level 4, equivalent to approx. grade 5)**

To move this answer into Levels 5 and 6, the candidate needs more detailed analysis, greater use of subject terminology, more extensive use of quotation and more discussion of context.

Sample Answer 2

This passage gives a powerfully symbolic account of Jane's status as an outsider. She has been locked in a room, separated from the rest of the family. The room is 'chill' and 'silent', the literal imagery becoming figurative as the room reflects how she perceives the family and society.[1] There is a 'week's quiet dust' which shows the room is neglected and has no life in it. In the last sentence of the first paragraph Brontë mentions the 'secret' that makes it 'lonely'. The short second paragraph tells us it is where her uncle died and where he lay in his coffin.[2] She has been cast out into the darkness with her dead uncle, whom she wants to believe would have been kinder to her. The older Jane, the narrator, recreates the feelings of her younger self, as she is in a situation which will haunt her throughout the novel. From the start the sympathetic reader sees her as she sees herself: alone and unjustly treated.[3]

In the third paragraph she describes the room in detail, its 'vacant majesty' perhaps reflecting the emptiness of the wealthy family and society in which Jane moves. Jane sees herself in the mirror – a 'strange little figure'.[4] Even at this age she sees herself as odd and different. She calls herself 'it' – as if even she does not have feelings for herself. She distances herself from her image, standing outside and analysing herself as she does throughout the narrative. She describes herself as 'half fairy, half imp'. Is she saying that she is so far outside society that she is like a changeling, a creature from another world? Imps are mischievous creatures, reflecting the way Mrs Reed sees her, but fairies have more positive connotations, so perhaps she is saying she doesn't mind being different.[5] After their first meeting, Rochester compares her to a fairy with a 'look of another world' and thinks that she has 'bewitched' his horse – or more likely him.

Throughout the novel she refers to herself as odd, small and not good looking.[6] She constantly compares herself unfavourably to others, associating conventional good looks with wealth and success in society. The tall, beautiful Blanche Ingram is the opposite of Jane and the ultimate 'insider'. However, the idea that she is an outsider in society is challenged by the events of her life. Lowood is a cruel place at first and reinforces her idea that she is a victim of society, as both education and religion are twisted into means of oppression. But by the time she leaves, Jane is an accomplished teacher, surely an insider at least at Lowood.[7] It is true that her position as a governess at Thornfield is an awkward one. She does not belong with the guests or with the servants. She sits watching the party but not joining in. On the other hand, Mrs Fairfax is kind to her and Rochester not only treats her well but falls in love with her. Perhaps she feels like an outsider because she is not admitted to the sort of upper or upper middle class society to which she feels she belongs. She most certainly is not as much of an outsider as Bertha Mason, whose madness causes her to be locked in the attic in a terrifyingly Gothic version of Jane's imprisonment in the red-room.[8]

When Jane leaves Thornfield, she is literally an outsider, cast out on the streets – but it might be noted that this is her choice, arising from her strong moral principles. She is welcomed into a comfortable home by the Rivers family and it is she who rejects St John's offer of marriage, again choosing to reject the conventions of society in favour of her own feelings and principles.[9] When she

> *returns to the blinded Rochester he too can be seen as an outsider, cutting himself off from society, and finding happiness with another outsider. However, when she reflects on her life at the end of the novel and declares triumphantly 'Reader, I married him', the reader must conclude that, if she ever was truly an outsider, she certainly is not now as she embarks on a happy marriage to a very rich man.*[10]

[1] An immediate thoughtful response to the question and a clear explanation of the writer's methods, supported by quotation and using appropriate subject terminology (AO2).

[2] Understanding of structure shown (AO2).

[3] This is much more coherent, focused on the question and showing insightful understanding of the writer's methods (AO1/AO2).

[4] Good use of quotation and explanation of the effects of language, tied to a consideration of context (AO1/AO2/AO3).

[5] Detailed analysis of the writer's methods, focused on question and considering alternative interpretations (AO1/AO2).

[6] The candidate has moved well to a consideration of the whole text, linking it with the contents of the extract (AO1/AO2).

[7] Critical and exploratory argument related to contextual factors (AO1/AO3).

[8] Convincing exploration of contextual factors, both historical and literary (AO3).

[9] The candidate is addressing the question in a critical and exploratory way, weighing up 'how far' she can be seen as an outsider, referring to incidents in the novel (AO1).

[10] The candidate arrives at a conclusion which is personal and well-argued, answering the question convincingly, while continuing to analyse the writer's methods (AO1/AO2/AO3).

- AO1: Critical, exploratory and well-structured approach to the task and whole text, supported by well-chosen references. 11 / 12 (Level 6)
- AO2: Detailed and sometimes insightful analysis of language, form and structure, using well-chosen and accurate terminology, exploring the effects of the writer's techniques on the audience. 11 / 12 (Level 6)
- AO3: Convincing exploration of different ideas and perspectives, linked to context. 6 / 6 (Level 6)

Mark ▶ **28 / 30 (Level 6, equivalent to approx. grade 8–9)**

 For more on the topics covered in this chapter, see pages 72–79 of the Collins AQA English Language & Literature Revision Guide.

English Literature Paper 2

* Modern Prose or Drama

The Exam

Paper 2 takes 2 hours and 15 minutes and there are three sections, so you should aim to spend no more than 45 minutes on Modern Prose or Drama (Section A).

There will be a total of 24 questions, two on each of the 12 set books:
* *An Inspector Calls* by J.B. Priestley
* *Blood Brothers* by Willy Russell
* *The History Boys* by Alan Bennett
* *DNA* by Dennis Kelly
* *The Curious Incident of the Dog in the Night-Time* by Simon Stephens
* *A Taste of Honey* by Shelagh Delaney
* *Lord of the Flies* by William Golding
* *Telling Tales* (the AQA Anthology)
* *Animal Farm* by George Orwell
* *Never Let Me Go* by Kazuo Ishiguro
* *Anita and Me* by Meera Syal
* *Pigeon English* by Stephen Kelman

You will probably have studied only one of these texts, either prose or drama, so you will have a choice between two questions. There will be no extracts from the text. Each question will be followed by two bullet points. The first bullet point focuses on the content of the text in terms of themes, ideas and characters (AO1) and the second on the writer's methods (AO2).

Skills Assessed in the Modern Prose or Drama Section

Like both sections of Paper 1, this section assesses your understanding of your ability to analyse the text that you have studied in class. You should have studied:
* the themes and characters of the text
* the writer's use of language
* form and structure
* the relationship of the text to its context.

You will be assessed on the same Assessment Objectives and against the same mark scheme as for Shakespeare. See page 68 for details of AO1, AO2, AO3 and AO4.

Drama: Character

There is a very good chance that one of the questions will focus on the characters from the play. As with Shakespeare in Paper 1, the question could focus on an aspect of the character or a way in which the character is used.

For example:
How does Stephens use Ed to explore ideas about being a parent in *The Curious Incident of the Dog in the Night-Time*?

Write about:
- what sort of a parent Ed is to Christopher
- how Stephens presents him as a parent in the play.

Alternatively, the focus could be on a relationship between two or more characters.

For example:
Towards the end of *The History Boys*, Akthar says that 'there was a contract' between Hector and the boys. What do you think he means by this?

Write about:
- whether you think there is a 'contract' and, if so, what it is
- how Bennett presents the relationship between Hector and the boys.

As you can see above, each question will be followed by two bullet points – the first bullet point will encourage you to stay focused on the question and the second will invite you to discuss the writer's methods.

Top Tip

Try to refer to the question – in a subtle way – in every paragraph of your answer.

Characters in modern drama are presented in much the same way as characters in Shakespeare. This is done by these means:

What they say and how they say it	In some modern plays, such as *The History Boys* and *The Curious Incident of the Dog in the Night-Time*, characters speak directly to the audience as they sometimes do in Shakespeare. Others, like *A Taste of Honey*, employ the convention of 'the **fourth wall**', meaning that there can be no contact between actors and audience. All characters reveal themselves in dialogue. The characters in *An Inspector Calls* tell us a lot about themselves as they tell the Inspector of their relationships with Eva Smith. Russell presents class differences in *Blood Brothers* partly through the way in which his characters speak.
What they do	In *Blood Brothers* Mrs Johnstone's action in giving away Edward can be interpreted in different ways, as can Linda's actions in going to Edward for help. The characters in *DNA* are defined and shaped by what they do to cover up their crime.
What other characters say to or about them	In *The Curious Incident of the Dog in the Night-Time*, you can learn a lot about Christopher from his parents and Siobhan. You get different points of view about Hector in *The History Boys* from teachers and pupils.
How other characters react to them	The 'love–hate' relationship between Jo and Helen is at the centre of *A Taste of Honey*. They inspire strong and contradictory feelings in each other.

In many modern plays you can also learn about characters from stage directions. These are chiefly intended for directors and actors to help them interpret the play in the way the writer intended. How much guidance is given varies from writer to writer and influences the amount of freedom actors have to interpret characters in different ways. J.B. Priestley gives lengthy descriptions of appearance and character:

ARTHUR BIRLING *is a heavy-looking, rather portentous man in his middle fifties with fairly easy manners but rather provincial in his speech.*

Shelagh Delaney's directions are briefer but just as significant:

Enter PETER, *a brash car salesman, cigar in mouth.*

Brief quotations from the stage directions can be very useful in writing about characters.

Drama: Themes and Ideas

Themes, ideas and issues are often explored through characters, so you will be discussing them whatever the question. However, some questions will refer directly to themes, ideas and issues:

- How does Priestley explore ideas about responsibility in *An Inspector Calls*?
- It has been said that *DNA* presents a disturbing picture of modern youth. How far do you agree?

In some modern plays, themes and issues are very much to the fore. *The Curious Incident of the Dog in the Night-Time* is usually seen as a play about autism but, interestingly, 'autism' is never mentioned in the play. This suggests that the writer wants us to look beyond labels and to see Christopher as an individual. Nevertheless, to see it simply as a play about a boy who is unusual would be very naïve. One has to ask whether, if it were not for the autism issue, it would be of any interest.

DNA and *Blood Brothers* also have overarching 'issues', which some might think are presented in a fairly simplistic way. The former is about guilt and responsibility, touching on similar issues to those of *An Inspector Calls*; the latter is primarily about class issues. It is harder to discern strong issues in *A Taste of Honey* and *The History Boys*. Neither of these plays is at all 'preachy', as others might sometimes be, but they do make their audiences think about the themes and ideas they touch on.

To gain high marks in an English Literature paper, you are expected to analyse and evaluate the text. It is always good to discuss alternative viewpoints and interpretations. At first sight this might not always seem possible with the set plays. Most readers and audiences would probably conclude that:

- *An Inspector Calls* is all about the fact that 'we are all responsible for each other'
- *Blood Brothers* tells us that our lives are shaped by the social class in which we are brought up
- *DNA* is about how alienated young people are from society and what this can lead to
- *The Curious Incident of the Dog in the Night-Time* tells us that people with autism are valuable members of society.

However, remember that every member of every audience reacts in his or her own way to a piece of theatre. Some of them might think that:

- *An Inspector Calls* shows us how selfish people were in 1912, but they are no different now so it was naïve of Priestley to think we can be responsible for each other

- In *Blood Brothers*, Mrs Johnstone and Mickey are responsible for their own problems – it is not inevitable that she gets into debt or he gets involved with crime
- *DNA* is the sordid story of some quite unappealing teenagers about whom it is difficult to care
- *The Curious Incident of the Dog in the Night-Time* does not ask deep enough questions about why Christopher is as he is.

Such opinions may be controversial and if you are going to express them in an exam you need to be able to take more conventional views into account, argue your point of view convincingly and make sure everything you say is backed up by evidence from the text.

The History Boys is more open to interpretation. Is it about an inspiring but misunderstood teacher? Is it about a pompous failure who sexually abuses his pupils? Is it saying that in the end it really does not matter what the teacher is like or how many exams you pass? It could be about all these things and many more.

A Taste of Honey is much more difficult to discuss in terms of ideas and issues. It is essentially about one girl and her relationships but it touches on ideas about class, parenthood, sexual attraction and being an outsider in society. It is very much of its time, reflecting the concerns and attitudes of the 1950s.

Top Tip

On the Internet, look up reviews of the play you have studied (if you have studied a novel, you can do the same thing) and compare how different reviewers have reacted to it.

Context

There is a separate mark for context but the exam board is very keen that it should be considered naturally as part of your answer, not 'bolted on'. What does this mean in practice?

- <u>Do not</u> write a paragraph about 'history':

An Inspector Calls was written in the 1940s but set in 1912 before the First World War. After the war, society changed significantly. The play was first performed just after the Second World War. Britain elected a Labour government and they brought in the National Health Service. Priestley was a socialist who supported this.

English Literature Paper 2

This is true – and it is important that you know it – but it should inform your answer, not be a separate part of it.

- <u>Do</u> use your knowledge of context within your answer:

The Inspector's reference to 'fire and blood and anguish' can be seen as a direct reference to the carnage of the First World War, which started just a couple of years after the time when the play was set and radically changed society. The play's first audiences might also have thought about the Second World War and what would happen in its aftermath. However, it can also be seen as a more general warning about how selfishness and greed can lead to revolution and chaos.

This discussion of context is rooted firmly in the text and is part of an analysis of the Inspector's speech. It would attract a good mark – but only if it is relevant to the question you have been asked.

Bear in mind that 'context' is not just about history and society. In the case of plays, you should think about the play's genre and style, and why and for whom it was written:
- *An Inspector Calls* is in the tradition of the 'well-made' three-act play, apparently **naturalistic** and employing the convention of the 'fourth wall'.
- *Blood Brothers* was originally written as a small-scale play to be toured to schools. It retains some of the 'broad brush' simplicity of that style but in its current form it follows the conventions of musical theatre, for example using songs to express strong emotions.
- *The History Boys* uses '**Brechtian**' techniques, such as characters 'stepping out' of the action and addressing the audience, which have become the norm in contemporary theatre.
- *DNA* was written to be performed by young people in schools or colleges. This influences its simple staging and its range of characters.
- *The Curious Incident of the Dog in the Night-Time* was adapted from a novel for the West End theatre. Like *The History Boys* it employs Brechtian techniques. It also uses a lot of impressive visual 'tricks'.
- *A Taste of Honey* belongs to a genre known as 'kitchen sink drama', when stories about working-class people were brought to the stage in the 1950s and 1960s. While the subject matter might have been considered very modern, the style is traditional and naturalistic.

> **Top Tip**
>
> Find out more about the background of your play and the traditions it comes from. Think about how that influences the contents of the play and its effect on the audience.

Drama: Language, Form and Structure

As there is no extract reproduced in the paper, you will not be able to do the sort of close analysis expected in other sections of the Literature exam. However, you still need to comment on language. You should consider the kind of language used by different characters and what this says about them and the themes of the play. You may wish to comment on these points:

- **Dialect** / regional speech patterns
  In *Blood Brothers* many, but importantly not all, of the characters speak with a Liverpool accent, which Russell conveys to some extent by changing the spelling of certain words, and use some regional words and expressions, as well as grammatical patterns. Similarly, the characters in *A Taste of Honey* use the speech patterns and characteristic expressions of Lancashire:

I'd sooner be put on't streets

- **Slang**
  DNA is not set in a specific place but the characters use non-standard language typical of teenagers. Some of the language of *Blood Brothers* and *A Taste of Honey* could also be described as slang (the concepts of dialect and slang overlap), as can some of the language used by younger characters in *An Inspector Calls:*

It's a rotten shame

- Use of Standard English
  Standard English is the norm for all characters in *An Inspector Calls*, as it is in *The History Boys.* In these plays, as in *Blood Brothers*, the use of Standard English reflects the characters' social status and/or their situation.

- **Idiolect** (the characteristic speech of an individual)
  Writers sometimes give characters their own quirks of speech. Christopher in *The Curious Tale of the Dog in the Night-Time* has a very particular, rather formal yet plain style of speech:

> *Father was angry. He grabbed me so I hit him and then we had a fight.*

- Heightened or poetic language
  Playwrights often use more poetic language, particularly imagery, at times of heightened emotion, such as the Inspector's final speech in *An Inspector Calls* or the narrator's speeches in *Blood Brothers*. Characters in *The History Boys* consciously employ complex literary or academic language:

> *At which point the Hun, if I may so characterise the fair Fiona, suddenly dug in, no further deployments were sanctioned, and around 23.00 hours our forces withdrew.*

When thinking about form and structure, consider the following:
- How the play's form is influenced by theatrical traditions and fashions.
- How it is divided – two or three long acts, the action of each being continuous and in one place, as in *A Taste of Honey* and *An Inspector Calls*, or a series of short scenes jumping from one time and one place to another?
- The story structure (Is there much exposition? Where are the turning points? What is the climax? What is the denouement? Are there twists and surprises?).
- Whether there are any unusual or interesting structural devices, for example the use of the narrator in *Blood Brothers* or the characters in *The History Boys* stepping out from the past to address the audience.

Modern Prose

You should approach your modern prose text in the same way as your 19th century novel (see pages 83–96). You will not, however, be given an extract from the text so there will not be the same degree of close analysis. In answering the question, make sure that you write about the whole text. If you have studied the AQA Anthology, each of the two questions will name a story from the anthology and ask you to answer the question about that story and one other story. Because the same mark scheme applies to all the set texts, there are no marks given for comparing the two stories, so while the board says that a structured comparison is 'permitted' it is unlikely – however skilful – to earn you extra marks. So you can, in effect, write two separate short essays.

Prose: Character and Voice

An understanding of the narrative voice is essential and the writer's choice of narrative voice and style is important:

- The narrators of *Lord of the Flies* and *Animal Farm* are detached, omniscient narrators.
- The first-person narrators of *Anita and Me*, *Pigeon English* and *Never Let Me Go* display varying degrees of naïvety and reliability. *Pigeon English* features a rather odd second narrative voice (the pigeon).
- *Telling Tales* features a range of narrative styles.

In the first-person narratives, other characters are seen through the eyes of the narrator but not always with the same effect:

- In *Anita and Me*, Meena, looking back on her childhood, would appear to be giving a reliable account of people and events, though she does admit to being 'a liar' and some readers may not warm to her or her opinions.
- Harry in *Pigeon English* is naïve and often mistaken. We see other characters as he sees them.
- Kathy in *Never Let Me Go* appears to be a confident, reliable narrator at first but it becomes clear that there are many things she does not understand, including how other characters feel about her.
- Much of the action in *Lord of the Flies* is seen through Ralph's eyes but the omniscient narrator also shares the thoughts and feelings of others. At times characters are symbolic but they can also be complex and psychologically convincing.
- Characters in *Animal Farm* are 'types', broadly drawn in keeping with a **fable**. As it is an **allegory** of the Russian Revolution, some represent historical figures and others represent groups or classes of people.

Prose: Themes and Context

When you write about the themes, ideas and issues in your text you will also, quite naturally, write about their context:

- *Anita and Me* is about growing up, belonging and experiencing racism. These themes and the context of the Midlands in the 1960s and 70s are woven together in the story.
- Similarly, *Pigeon English* is all about the experience of growing up and experiencing violence in a contemporary urban environment. The context shapes the characters and the story.
- An understanding of the science fiction genre helps with *Never Let Me Go*. Science fiction often uses ideas about what might happen in the future or in an alternative version of the present.

- *Lord of the Flies* uses some of the conventions of the boys' adventure story to explore issues about contemporary society. Golding particularly drew on *Treasure Island.*
- *Animal Farm* can be described as a fable, a fairy story or an allegory. Orwell uses an apparently simple form to look at ideas about power, equality and freedom.
- The short stories in *Telling Tales* are all rooted in the time when they were written and tend to focus on one aspect of the society of that time, for example the effect of a working man's death on his wife in the 'Odour of Chrysanthemums' or the return of a Japanese son from abroad in 'A Family Supper'.

Prose: Language and Structure

If your novel or story is first-person narrative, think about the language used by the narrator and its register, particularly the degree of formality or informality and whether the narrator uses Standard English. This influences the tone of the novel and the narrator's relationship with the reader. The narrators in *Anita and Me* and *Never Let Me Go* write as if they are looking back on their lives from a more mature standpoint – they are writing in Standard English but in quite an intimate, chatty tone. *Pigeon English* is very informal, written as if Harry is speaking to the reader directly in his own register.

Both third-person and first-person narratives use different registers to 'place' characters in terms of their region, age and social class. Piggy in *Lord of the Flies* has speech patterns that reflect the difference in class between him and the other boys. The pigs in *Animal Farm* adopt a formal way of speaking associated with authority.

Most of the novels and stories are structured conventionally, in chronological order, but you should take note of any unusual aspects of structure and think about their effect on the reader, such as the italicised speech at the beginning of each chapter in *Pigeon English*. Look for the key moments in the novel – turning points when things change – and the effect of these on characters (especially the protagonist) and plot.

> **Top Tip**
>
> All stories, whether in drama or prose, have a similar structure, which can be analysed in different ways:
>
> Exposition – inciting incident – one or more turning points – climax – denouement
> Or
> Exposition – conflict – turning point – climax – resolution – denouement
>
> Try analysing the story of your text according to both these models.

Worked Example

See page 3 for suggestions on how to make effective use of the worked example.

J.B. Priestley: *An Inspector Calls*

How does Priestley use the character of Inspector Goole to explore issues about responsibility in *An Inspector Calls*?

Write about:
- what the Inspector does and says
- how Priestley presents ideas through him by the way he writes.   [30 marks]
                                                                          AO4 [4 marks]

This question is about a character but it also focuses on a theme (responsibility). It is important that the focus of your answer remains on both the character and the issue. Starting the question with 'how' directs you to write about the writer's techniques. This is reinforced by the second bullet point. The bullet points indicate that you are being assessed on AO1 and AO2 equally but you should not separate the two. An answer that separated 'what' and 'how' would look odd. The 'how' should be considered along with the 'what', as should the context.

Below is an answer that should achieve Level 4 (about grade 5). To remind yourself of the requirements of Levels 4, 5 and 6, refer to page 78.

Sample Answer 1

The Inspector comes to investigate a crime and he questions all the other characters about Eva Smith and whether they are responsible for her death. He is called 'Inspector Goole', which sounds a bit like 'ghoul' so maybe he is a ghost from the future. We do not know much about him and when Birling makes enquiries no-one has heard of him so perhaps he was not sent by the police and is something supernatural sent to make the Birlings look at themselves.[1]

He does not accuse anyone of killing Eva and from the start he says she has killed herself so he is not really investigating a crime in the normal way, although he acts just like a policeman in a detective story. He is finding out how each of the characters knew her and how their actions drove her to suicide. He wants them to take responsibility.[2] He asks Arthur Birling about why he sacked the girl and Birling says he has 'nothing whatever to do' with the girl's death but the Inspector disagrees and mentions a 'chain of events'.[3] This chain of events continued when Sheila had her sacked from a job in a shop because she was jealous of her. Up till now Sheila has been more sympathetic to Eva than the others and when she realises that she too could be responsible she feels 'rotten' and asks 'so I'm responsible?' This contrasts with her father's reaction.[4] Sheila then realises that her fiancé Gerald had an affair with Eva. He says he feels 'ashamed' so he takes some responsibility. At the end of the first act Sheila tells Gerald that they cannot hide anything because the Inspector 'knows'. The audience might wonder what else he knows and, if he already knows, why is he asking questions?[5]

In the next act the Inspector questions Mrs Birling. She turned the girl away from a charity but will not take any responsibility. She says the girl had 'no-one to blame but herself' for being pregnant and having no money but she then blames the child's father. The climax of the act is when the Inspector, knowing the father is her son Eric, forces her to say he is responsible.[6]

By his questioning the Inspector makes the other characters look at their consciences and think about responsibility.[7] The young people are more willing to accept responsibility than the parents, which might be Priestley saying there is hope for the future because the things the Inspector says make it clear he is not just talking about one girl's death.[8] He says there are 'millions of Eva Smiths' and 'We are all responsible for each other'. The Inspector leaves having blamed everybody for Eva's death. He has also made the audience think about society in general and how they might be responsible for things that happen in the world.[9]

---

[1] A reasonable attempt to respond to the question but perhaps a little confused and unclear – the part about the ghost is not linked to the question (AO1).

[2] Clearer explanation. Explains how the character is used to explore responsibility (AO1/AO2).

[3] Uses quotations effectively, though there is not much analysis (AO1).

[4] Clear understanding of the text shown with appropriate textual reference (AO1).

[5] Clear explanation of the effect of the play's structure on the audience (AO2).

[6] Good use of textual reference and clear understanding of the text. The candidate is thinking about 'responsibility' (AO1).

[7] Focus is brought back to the question and the 'how' is considered – 'by his questioning' (AO1/AO2).

[8] Good understanding of the text and Priestley's ideas shown (AO1/AO2/AO3).

[9] Shows a secure grasp of the play's themes and context, supported by appropriate quotations (AO1/AO3).

- AO1: The response is clear and fairly consistent, but sometimes strays from the question and tends to re-tell the story without much analysis. There is clear focus on the issue of responsibility throughout but not so much on the Inspector. There is a range of reference, short appropriate quotations being used throughout. 7 / 12 (Lower Level 4)
- AO2: Some clear explanation of the writer's methods, including comments on language structure, but lacks clear comment on language. There is not much relevant subject terminology. 6 / 12 (Upper Level 3)
- AO3: Context is considered clearly in the last paragraph and there is an implied awareness of it in terms of the Inspector's role throughout. 4 / 6 (Level 4)
- AO4: 3 / 4

Mark 20 / 34 (Level 4, equivalent to approx. grade 5)

To move this answer into Levels 5 and 6, the candidate needs detailed analysis, greater use of subject terminology and more discussion of context.

Sample Answer 2

The Inspector is introduced as a conventional, stock character such as we would expect to see in a murder mystery or a detective story. He is a high-ranking policeman who has been sent to a middle class home to investigate a crime. However, as the play progresses we realise he is not such a conventional figure and when Birling makes enquiries no-one has heard of him. He wants to know who is responsible for the death yet he is not looking for a murderer. The Inspector's idea of being responsible is much more than 'who dunnit?'[1]

As we would expect from a policeman, he is polite to Mr Birling, calling him 'sir' and asking him to help 'if you don't mind'. However, he is not as deferential as Mr Birling would like, insisting on doing his professional duty 'one person and one line of enquiry at a time' and responding to objections directly and firmly. It is his 'duty to ask questions' and he is established as a conscientious officer whose sense of duty sets him apart from the other characters. Unlike his boss, who plays golf with Arthur, he is not part of the Birlings' circle. He is interested only in the truth. As he discovers how each of the characters knew Eva and how their actions affected her, it becomes evident that he wants them to take responsibility.[2] When

Arthur Birling protests that he has 'nothing whatever to do' with the girl's death the Inspector disagrees and mentions a 'chain of events'. This chain of events continued when Sheila had her sacked from a job in a shop for a 'silly' reason. Sheila feels 'rotten' about her actions. Admitting some responsibility contrasts with her father's reaction, though her language suggests a certain childishness and ignorance of the world. [3] Her fiancé Gerald, admitting to an affair with Eva, says he feels 'ashamed' so he takes some responsibility – at least for betraying Sheila. Simply by being present the Inspector has caused him to become more honest and think about responsibility. At the end of the first act Sheila tells Gerald that they cannot hide anything because the Inspector 'knows', leaving the audience to wonder what else he knows and, if he already knows, why is he asking questions? [4]

The Inspector's questioning is insistent but not aggressive. In the second act he interjects short questions as Gerald gives his account of things – 'Where did you go?' 'Did she drink much?' – helping Gerald to open up. The device of having a policeman asking questions reveals to the audience the sort of life a man like Gerald might have led at the time and how, without meaning to do any harm, he has formed a link of the 'chain'. Mrs Birling, too, reveals her true nature under the Inspector's persistent questioning and falls into a trap he has set for her. Having said Eva/Daisy has 'only herself to blame' she then blames the 'drunken young idler' who has got her pregnant. This comes at the climax of the act, which is full of dramatic irony as everyone else realises that the 'idler' is her son, Eric, and the Inspector, remaining calm in contrast to the hysterical, broken family, waits calmly 'to do my duty'. [5]

In the third act, we reach the denouement when, as in a detective story, the Inspector apportions blame: 'each of you helped to kill her'. He is now doing most of the talking, and his language becomes more emotive as he talks about how Eva/Daisy was treated 'as if she were an animal'. [6] Finally, he makes his speech about 'millions of Eva Smiths'. By doing this he opens up the idea of responsibility.

The play has not just been about one woman's death. Indeed it is never certain whether all the characters are talking about the same girl. Now we see that Eva Smith could have been any one of millions of working class people who have been harmed by the actions of people like the Birlings. The Inspector's statement that 'We are all responsible for each other' is addressed to the audience as much as to the family. [7] The Inspector is a dramatic device that enables the other characters to expose their lives to scrutiny. He is also a mysterious figure, perhaps from the *future, come to warn the Birlings and their class of the consequences of their actions. He promises 'fire and blood and anguish' if we do not take responsibility for each other. The strength of that warning is increased by his use of violent, almost biblical language – in contrast to his earlier plain, measured way of speaking – which makes him seem like a prophet to whom we must all listen.[8]*

[1] Already beginning to explore ideas thoughtfully – a perceptive link with context (AO1/AO3).

[2] Thoughtful and detailed, linked to context, supported by apt references, and with some examination of language (AO1/AO2/AO3).

[3] Detailed analysis of language linked to context (AO2/AO3).

[4] Thoughtful consideration of how the Inspector is used, showing understanding of structure, supported by appropriate references (AO1/AO2/AO3).

[5] Detailed examination of the writer's method, using subject terminology well, supported by well-chosen quotations and linked to context (AO1/AO2/AO3).

[6] Excellent focus on the question – thoughtful and well supported with quotations and subject terminology (AO1/AO2).

[7] A critical, exploratory consideration of the whole play, well focused on the use of responsibility (AO1/AO2/AO3).

[8] The whole essay has been coherent and exploratory. There is a strong sense of the effect of the writer's methods on the audience and specific detailed links with context (AO1/AO3).

- AO1: Critical, exploratory and conceptualised. Well focused on the task with very well-chosen references supporting the interpretation. One possible criticism is that there is no sense of alternative interpretations. 10 / 12 (Level 5)
- AO2: Interesting and sophisticated analysis of the writer's methods with an excellent use of subject terminology. Explores the effects of the writer's methods on the audience. 12 / 12 (Level 6)
- AO3: Detailed links between task and context as ideas and perspectives are effectively explored. 6 / 6 (Level 6)
- AO4: 4 / 4

Mark ▶ **32 / 34 (Level 6, equivalent to approx. grade 8–9)**

For more on the topics covered in this chapter, see pages 84–91 of the Collins AQA English Language & Literature Revision Guide.

The Exam

You should aim to spend no more than 45 minutes on the Poetry section of Paper 2 (Section B).

There will only be two questions – one on the 'Love and Relationships' section of the AQA Anthology *Poems Past and Present* and the other on the 'Power and Conflict' section. You will probably have studied only one of these sections, so will have no choice over which question to answer. Each question will name a poem from the anthology, which will be printed on the page. You will be asked to compare this poem to any other poem from your section of the anthology.

Skills Assessed in the Poetry Section

Like both sections of Paper 1 and Section A of Paper 2, the poetry section assesses your understanding of the texts that you have studied in class and your ability to analyse them. You should have studied:

- themes and ideas
- the writer's use of language
- form and structure
- the relationship of the poems to their context.

You will be assessed on AO1, AO2 and AO3. For details of the AOs, see page 68.

Themes and Ideas

The poems you have studied are grouped under a heading, either 'Love and Relationships' or 'Power and Conflict', so it is clear what the connecting theme of each group is. Think about:

- what aspects of the main theme appear in each poem
- what other ideas and themes the poet is concerned with
- how you can connect poems through their treatment of themes and ideas.

Because most poems are quite short, poets tend not to explore their themes in great depth or detail. They tend to focus on an incident or a moment, relating an anecdote or giving a kind of snapshot of someone's feelings. Poems that tell a story include 'Porphyria's Lover' and 'Bayonet Charge'. Sometimes the story is personal, giving rise to reflection and a consideration by the poet of its meaning, as in 'The Prelude'. It may describe an '**epiphany**', a key moment of revelation and understanding. Other poets, such as Browning, do not include their thoughts but allow readers to decide for themselves what the story might mean. Poems that do not tell a story usually focus on the poet's feelings. Poems like 'London' and 'Checking Out Me History' express strong views about their subject. Poems such as 'Winter Swans' and 'Ozymandias' work through imagery and description, leaving readers to infer the poet's attitudes and feelings.

Top Tip

You cannot always work out what the poet's attitude is. Poems can be **ambiguous** and sometimes obscure. The same poem can mean different things to different people. Your response and interpretation are as valid as anyone's.

Try to make connections between the poems in your cluster so that you are prepared to choose a poem to compare to the one given in the exam. Consider the following questions about each of your poems.

Love and Relationships

What sort of relationship is it?	• parents and children – 'Eden Rock' / 'Follower' • romantic love / passion – Sonnet 29 / 'Love's Philosophy' • marriage – 'Singh Song!' / 'The Farmer's Bride'
What else is the poem about?	• time passing – 'Neutral Tones' / 'Follower' • identity – 'Singh Song!' / 'Letters from Yorkshire' • death – 'Eden Rock' / 'Porphyria's Lover' • betrayal – 'Neutral Tones' / 'When We Two Parted' • nature – 'Winter Swans' / 'The Farmer's Bride' • parting – 'Walking Away' / 'When We Two Parted'
How does the poet or **persona** feel about the subject of the poem?	• passionate – 'Singh Song!' / 'Love's Philosophy' • possessive – 'Porphyria's Lover' / 'The Farmer's Bride' • protective – 'Walking Away' / 'Follower' • admiring – 'Before You Were Mine' / 'Climbing My Grandfather' • nostalgic – 'Eden Rock' / 'Follower' • angry / bitter – 'When We Two Parted' / 'Neutral Tones'

And how does the subject feel about the poet/persona?	• loving – 'Singh Song!' / 'Porphyria's Lover' • frightened – 'The Farmer's Bride' • indifferent – 'When We Two Parted' • protective – 'Follower' / 'Eden Rock' • or are the subject's feelings unknown?

Power and Conflict

What kind of power or conflict is it about?	• a war – 'The Charge of the Light Brigade' / 'War Photographer' • a psychological conflict – 'The Prelude' / 'Remains' • political power – 'Checking Out Me History' / 'London' • the power of an individual – 'Ozymandias' / 'My Last Duchess' • lack of power – 'The Émigrée' / 'Exposure'
What else is it about?	• loss – 'The Émigrée' / 'Poppies' • death – 'Exposure' / 'The Charge of the Light Brigade' • love – 'My Last Duchess' / 'Poppies' • nature – 'The Prelude' / 'Storm on the Island' • memory – 'The Prelude' / 'Tissue' • identity – 'The Émigrée' / 'Checking Out Me History'
How does the poet or persona feel?	• angry – 'London' / 'Checking Out Me History' • sad – 'War Photographer' / 'Poppies' • afraid – 'Bayonet Charge' / 'The Émigrée' • proud – 'The Charge of the Light Brigade' / 'Checking Out Me History' • awestruck – 'Storm on the Island '/ 'The Prelude' • confused – 'Kamikaze' / 'Remains' • thoughtful – 'Ozymandias' / 'Tissue'

> **Top Tip**
>
> Look on the Internet for interviews with, or articles by, the poets to gain an insight into their attitudes and why they may have written the poems.

Character and Voice

You should think about who is speaking, who is being addressed and who is being described. Poems are very often written in the first person. Unless you have reason to believe otherwise, you can usually assume that the 'I' of a poem is the poet. However, poets sometimes adopt a persona, writing 'in role' as a character. This is the norm in 'Power and Conflict', whereas most of the 'Love and Relationships' poems appear to be personal.

Poems often express poets' thoughts and emotions, giving us a window into their hearts and minds:

I have had worse partings, but none that so

Gnaws at my mind still.   ('Walking Away')

Here C. Day Lewis sums up his feelings at seeing his son walk into school. He seems to be trying to explain to us and to himself why such an everyday, common experience had such an effect on him. In 'Eden Rock' Charles Causley also shares personal experience and emotion with the reader, but most of the other 'Love and Relationships' poems are addressed to an individual – the object of the poet's emotions – and the reader might feel almost like an intruder. Elizabeth Barrett Browning is completely wrapped up in her feelings for the loved one:

My thoughts do twine and bud

About thee,   (Sonnet 29)

And Thomas Hardy expresses his bitterness to his former lover:

The smile on your mouth was the deadest thing.   ('Neutral Tones')

Poems where the poet adopts a persona are less often addressed to individuals. 'My Last Duchess' is an exception and here the addressee is not the object of the speaker's emotions. These poems tend to work more as inner monologues where we (and the poet) enter other people's minds to try to understand more about their lives. Browning was fascinated by the psychology of power and violence, giving a chilling insight into the mind of Porphyria's lover, while Armitage uses the first person to explore the psychological damage of war in 'Remains':

He's here in my head when I close my eyes. ('Remains')

In 'Ozymandias' Shelley uses the first person to introduce another speaker, the 'traveller from an antique land', who in turn tells the story of Ozymandias. So, far from making the poem more personal, the two voices serve to distance the story, making it myth-like. In 'Kamikaze' Garland starts in the third person, making the poem seem objective and distanced before finally giving a voice to her character. Tennyson tells the story of the Light Brigade in the third person but at the end his own voice intrudes, telling us to 'Honour the Light Brigade'. 'War Photographer' recounts its story in the third person with no comment from the poet and no direct voice given to the war photographer himself.

Top Tip

A 'persona' is a first person character adopted by the poet. Longer poems, such as Browning's, which are narrated by a persona are sometimes referred to as **dramatic monologues**.

Form and Structure

Some poems follow strict, traditional forms. They are regular, meaning they adhere to rules or patterns. Amongst the most common traditional forms of poetry are the **sonnet** and the **ballad**. Barrett Browning's Sonnet 29 is a **Petrarchan** (or Italian) sonnet in form. Shelley's 'Ozymandias' is a sonnet in some respects: it has fourteen lines and is written in iambic pentameter. However, the rhyme scheme diverts from the norm for a sonnet and the subject matter is unusual – traditionally sonnets are love poems. Ballads are traditionally folk songs or poems that tell a story, usually in regular four-line **stanzas** (**quatrains**). Hardy's 'Neutral Tones' and Blake's 'London' use variations of the ballad form.

Poetry that has a regular **metre** (see page 118) but no rhyme scheme is called blank verse. Poetry that has no regular pattern, either of metre or rhyme, is called **free verse**.

Stanzas

'Stanza' is Italian for room, so you could say that if the poem is a house, the stanzas are its rooms. You may also see stanzas referred to as verses, though that term is best avoided in literary criticism as it can also refer to a line of verse. Strictly speaking, in order to be described as stanzas, subdivisions of a poem should be regular in form and of equal length. Otherwise they should be referred to as 'verse paragraphs'. However, it is quite acceptable to use the word 'stanza' for any subdivision of a poem.

The following poems in the anthology do include regular stanzas of equal length: 'When We Two Parted'; 'Love's Philosophy'; 'Neutral Tones'; 'London'; 'Exposure'; 'Walking Away'; 'Follower'.

Interestingly, all these poems are about strong emotions. You might expect poets to use irregular verse to convey the strength of their emotions, showing that they have lost control. Perhaps organising their thoughts in strict patterns helps them to make sense of them. You should consider how such tension between form and content affects the impact of the poems on the reader. Other poems, such as 'Eden Rock' and 'The Charge of the Light Brigade' are mainly regular but occasionally vary the number of lines per stanza. Think about when and why such variations occur. You should also think about the contents of each stanza and how the poem develops through the stanzas.

Do not neglect the internal structure of single stanza poems. Sonnet 29 can be divided into two parts, the octave (eight lines) and the sestet (six lines). The transition from the octave to the sestet is called a **volta** (meaning 'turn') and signifies a turn in the argument or mood. Browning's dramatic monologues are structured like short stories. In 'Climbing My Grandfather' the lack of divisions reflects the continuous nature of the action described.

> ## Top Tip
>
> Look for anything unusual or irregular in a poem's structure and think about why the poem is not completely regular. Equally, consider why a poem might be completely regular or follow a traditional form.

Rhyme

Rhyme is easy to spot but can be difficult to analyse. It can be used to help give order to a poem, to amuse or to deliver a strong message. The simplest form of rhyme is the rhyming couplet – the form often used by children when they write verse. Browning uses rhyming couplets throughout 'My Last Duchess', the apparent simplicity of the form perhaps reflecting the disingenuous way in which the speaker feigns innocence. The rhyming couplets of 'The Farmer's Bride' could reflect the simplicity and lack of understanding of the persona. In 'Checking Out Me History' Agard's use of rhyme complements the childishness of some of the language.

Ballads traditionally use an *abab* rhyme scheme (rhyming the first line with the third and the second with the fourth). This pattern is used by Byron, Shelley and Heaney. Hardy uses an *abba* rhyme scheme in the ballad-like 'Neutral Tones'. Other poets, such as Duffy and Day Lewis, use more complex or original rhyme schemes. Others might use rhyme occasionally for effect, sometimes within a line (internal rhyme). Many modern and contemporary poets use **half rhyme**, also known as **slant rhyme**, and **pararhyme**, where the final consonants sound the same but the preceding vowels differ slightly. In 'Follower' Heaney rhymes 'sock' with 'pluck', while Owen rhymes 'snow' and 'renew' in 'Exposure'. This softens the effect of the rhyme, often helping to create a gentler tone or perhaps (in the case of 'Exposure') a sense of unease.

Rhythm and Metre

The rhythm of a poem comes from its pattern of stressed and unstressed syllables, which normally becomes clear when you read the poem aloud. This pattern is known as metre and its analysis is called **scansion**. Some poetry, especially modern poetry, is very difficult to scan and it is not always helpful to try. However, it can be a useful way of describing a poem's rhythm and its effect if the metre used is mainly regular. Some poems, such as 'The Charge of the Light Brigade', have a strong regular rhythm:

Half a league, Half a league,

Half a league onward,   ('The Charge of the Light Brigade')

In this poem Tennyson mostly uses the **dactyl** (a stressed syllable followed by two unstressed syllables) and the **trochee** (a stressed syllable followed by one unstressed syllable), giving a sense of excitement and speed in keeping with his subject. Starting with the stressed syllable can give a sense of strength and confidence. The **spondee** (two stressed syllables) is especially strong but could not be used for a whole line of poetry.

Perhaps the most common metre in English is the iambic pentameter, as used by Shakespeare. The iamb (unstressed syllable followed by stressed syllable) is sometimes said to resemble the human heartbeat and reflect the natural rhythms of speech. Wordsworth uses it in 'The Prelude':

And, as I rose upon the stroke, my boat

Went heaving through the water like a swan   ('The Prelude')

The regular, gentle rhythm helps to create the mood of the poem. Poets sometimes vary their metre with **anapaests** (two unstressed followed by one stressed). Anapaests can help to create a lively, sometimes comic, mood.

Pentameter means that there are five 'feet' (units of metre) per line. 'Penta' is Greek for five so an iambic pentameter is a line of five iambs.

You might also come across:
- a dimeter (a line of two feet), as in 'The Charge of the Light Brigade'
- a trimeter (three feet), as in some lines of 'Love's Philosophy'
- a tetrameter (four feet), also in 'Love's Philosophy'
- a hexameter or alexandrine (six feet), as in 'Exposure'.

20th and 21st century poets are less likely to use strong metrical patterns. A poem such as 'Eden Rock' does have an underlying metre but it is not regular and so sounds more like everyday speech. 'Checking Out Me History', on the other hand, has a very strong rhythm, reflecting the poet's speech as he reads it aloud or recites it.

> **Top Tip**
>
> While some poems have regular unchanging metrical patterns, others will change the pattern from stanza to stanza or line to line, perhaps even for a single foot (for example starting a line with a trochee rather than an iamb). Think about why the metre might change and what effect the change has on the reader.

Language

The poet Coleridge described poetry as 'the best words in the best possible order'. Every word counts and you must think about why the poets have chosen the words they have.

Sound

The sound of a poem is created by its rhythm and rhyme and by the sound of the words. In poetry, sound and meaning are inextricably linked. The most obvious way in which sound reflects meaning is through onomatopoeia, when a word sounds like its meaning. In Sonnet 29, Barrett Browning uses the word 'rustle' to convey the sound of the wind in the trees. Alliteration, where a succession of words start with, or include, the same consonant sound, can convey different moods by the sound used. Alliteration of 's' (also known as **sibilance**) is sometimes used to express a sinister, dangerous feeling, as in 'Exposure':

> Sudden successive flights of bullets streak the silence.   ('Exposure')

Browning uses plosive sounds to create an unsettling mood in 'Porphyria's Lover':

> Blushed bright beneath my burning kiss.   ('Porphyria's Lover')

The letters 'p' and 'b' have an explosive quality, while 'd','t', 'k' and 'g' tend to sound quite hard. 'S' and 'sh' are soft, with a hissing quality. Poets also sometimes use a series of vowel sounds for effect, which is known as assonance. Wordsworth uses three long 'o' sounds in this line from 'The Prelude' to give a sense of the regularity and perhaps the effort of rowing:

> And, as I rose upon the stroke, my boat   ('The Prelude')

Poets often repeat whole words and phrases, not just sounds. In 'The Charge of the Light Brigade' anaphora (repeating the word 'cannon' at the start of each line) combines with rhythm to create a sense of urgency and excitement:

> Cannon to right of them,
>
> Cannon to left of them,
>
> Cannon in front of them   ('The Charge of the Light Brigade')

 Top Tip

To help you to understand the effect of a poet's use of sound, read the poem out loud and/or listen to someone else reading it. On the Internet you will be able to find recordings of some of the anthology poems being read by the writers.

Diction

Diction, like register, refers to a writer's choice of vocabulary. Most of the poems you have studied are written in Standard English but sometimes poets use non-standard forms to reflect the way their personae would speak, as in 'Singh Song!' In this poem, words are spelled to convey the speaker's accent, giving a comic effect but also drawing attention to his ethnic identity:

And he vunt me not to hav a break

But ven nobody in, I do di lock   ('Singh Song!')

In 'Remains', Armitage uses non-standard colloquial vocabulary and grammar to reflect the speech of the soldier. This helps to give a sense of the reality of the situation and, in a sense, its ordinariness:

And one of them legs it up the road,   ('Remains')

Diction also reflects the subject matter of the poem, as in 'Follower'. This use of specialist vocabulary, which would be unfamiliar to most readers, conveys the poet's father's expertise and skill:

An expert. He would set the wing

And fit the bright steel-pointed sock.   ('Follower')

Imagery

Imagery refers to the way writers create pictures with their words. Literal imagery is the use of description to convey mood or atmosphere, reflecting the themes and ideas of the poem. Figurative imagery is the use of an image of one thing to tell us about another. The simplest form of figurative imagery is the simile, which makes a direct comparison between one thing and another, using a link word such as 'like' or 'as'. In 'The Farmer's Bride', the farmer uses a series of similes to describe his bride:

Shy as a leveret, swift as he,

Slight and straight as a young larch tree,

Sweet as the first wild violets, she,   ('The Farmer's Bride')

These similes reflect the character of the persona as well as his bride as they are part of his world, and make us see the bride as something wild.

A metaphor is a comparison that is implied. Rather than saying directly that one thing is like another, the writer describes it as if it were that thing. In 'When We Two Parted', Byron describes the sound of his ex-lover's name as 'a knell in mine ear', invoking connotations of death. Metaphors often describe parts of nature or abstract ideas as if they were people: this is called personification. In 'Exposure' the wind is described as 'merciless' and 'mad', while Tennyson writes of 'the jaws of Death'.

Symbols are objects that represent feelings or ideas. Often these are widely understood, like the poppies in the poem of the same name, but poets also create their own symbols. In 'Ozymandias' the broken statue becomes a symbol of the futility of power. The swans of 'Winter Swans' symbolise love and commitment as they 'mate for life'. Some poets take an image and develop it. Waterhouse does this in 'Climbing My Grandfather', using an extended metaphor of mountain climbing, as does Dharker in 'Tissue', though it is hard to define what the paper is meant to represent. In Sonnet 29, Barrett Browning develops the image of the vines around the tree to explain the quality of her love.

> ### Top Tip
>
> Look for patterns in the imagery of the poem, for example images of war or nature, and think about what this tells you about the themes and ideas of the poem.

Context

The themes explored in the poems are rooted in their historical, social and cultural contexts but this also holds true for their use of form, structure and language. References are often specific to time and place. The 'Thermos' and 'H.P. Sauce bottle' help to *place* 'Eden Rock' in a time and social context that would invoke memories in many older readers. Duffy's references in 'Before You Were Mine' have a similar effect. 'Follower' and 'Singh Song!' are also set in specific social situations, giving readers an insight into lives that may be different from theirs in terms of ethnicity, place or time.

To understand these poems it is not necessary to know a lot about their context, as it can be accessed easily through the poems. Many of the poems in the 'Power and

Conflict' section, however, might require a little bit of research into their historical contexts. Contemporary attitudes to the charge are reflected in 'The Charge of the Light Brigade', for example, which Tennyson wrote after reading about both the brigade's 'glory' and the fact that 'Some one had blunder'd'. 'Exposure' is the only war poem in the anthology written from personal experience and some understanding of Owen's life is helpful when studying it. It can also be helpful to find out more about the wars that inspired 'Kamikaze', 'Bayonet Charge', 'Remains' and 'War Photographer', though the latter two, like 'The Émigrée', could be about any modern conflict.

An understanding of literary traditions and movements is also useful. Several of the poets represented in the anthology (Blake, Wordsworth, Shelley and Byron) are Romantic poets. They were part of a poetic movement that rejected the classically inspired forms of the 18th century and the way intellectuals valued reason and logic above feelings. The Romantics used traditional, simpler forms such as the ballad. They sometimes wrote about ordinary people's lives and used more accessible language. Most of their poetry – both **lyric poetry** like 'Love's Philosophy' and longer works such as 'The Prelude' – focuses on nature, which they associated with human emotions and creativity. They could also be political, as in 'London', inspired by events such as the French Revolution.

You can see the influence of the Romantics in many later 19th century poets, such as Browning, Barrett Browning, Mew and Hardy. The 'modern' era of the early 20th century influenced poets to become more experimental and adventurous with both form and subject matter, but you can still see the influence of the Romantics in poems such as 'Follower', 'Winter Swans' and 'Letters from Yorkshire'.

Comparing Poems

Roughly half the marks awarded for AO1 are for the quality of your comparison between the two poems. When writing a comparison essay, it is important that you devote equal space to both poems and compare every aspect. You should be able to compare the poems' themes and ideas, structure and form, and use of language. Your comparisons should be informed by an understanding of their social, historical and cultural contexts.

Re-read the poem that you are given and think carefully about which poem to compare it with. Your choice will be limited by the focus of the question. For example, if the question is about parent–child relationships, your choice will be limited to a small number of poems. You will also be influenced by how well you know each poem. It is a good idea to choose a poem that you enjoy and can write enthusiastically about (you are also more likely to remember a poem you enjoy). Remember to look at similarities as well as differences.

Worked Example

See page 3 for suggestions on how to make effective use of the worked example.

Compare how poets present memories in 'Neutral Tones' and one other poem from 'Love and Relationships'. [30 marks]

Neutral Tones   *Thomas Hardy*

We stood by a pond that winter day,
And the sun was white, as though chidden of God,
And a few leaves lay on the starving sod;
– They had fallen from an ash, and were gray.

Your eyes on me were as eyes that rove   **5**
Over tedious riddles of years ago;
And some words played between us to and fro-
On which lost the more by our love.

The smile on your mouth was the deadest thing
Alive enough to have strength to die;   **10**
And a grin of bitterness swept thereby
Like an ominous bird a-wing…

Since then, keen lessons that love deceives,
And wrings with wrong, have shaped to me
Your face, and the God-curst sun, and a tree,   **15**
And a pond edged with grayish leaves.

The question is about 'memories' so first think about which other poems involve memories. You could certainly choose from: 'When We Two Parted'; 'Walking Away'; 'Eden Rock'; 'Follower'; 'Climbing My Grandfather'; 'Winter Swans'.

'Before You Were Mine' might also be said to be about memories, though they are either second-hand or imagined. You could also make a case for 'Mother, Any

Distance' and 'Letters from Yorkshire' being about memories but they are more about the poets' present situations than about looking back.

Look for similarities and differences between the poems.

'When We Two Parted' is about a similar situation with subtle differences in the poet's feelings. 'Winter Swans' is also about a lover or spouse, but with a happier outcome. All of the others are about relatives, not lovers and, despite a melancholy tone in all except 'Climbing My Grandfather', the memories described are generally happy ones. In all of them a remembered incident makes the poet think about passing time, change and even death. All except 'Climbing My Grandfather' are structured in a similar, mainly regular, way. They all use imagery and the sound of words to create their mood. 'Climbing My Grandfather' and 'Follower' perhaps have too little in common with 'Neutral Tones' and, conversely, 'When We Two Parted' has too much. 'Walking Away', 'Eden Rock' and 'Winter Swans' all provide plenty of material for a good comparison essay.

Top Tip

Make sure your choice of poem is appropriate for the task. If the question about 'Neutral Tones' focused on feelings about a lover rather than memories, you might use Sonnet 29, 'When We Two Parted' or 'Porphyria's Lover'. If the focus were the use of natural imagery then Sonnet 29, 'Love's Philosophy', 'Winter Swans' and 'Letters from Yorkshire' would all be appropriate choices.

To get a reasonably good mark (Level 4, the equivalent of grade 5), you need to show:

	AO1	AO2	AO3
Level 4 16–20 marks	• Clear comparisons • Effective use of references to support comparisons	• Clear explanation of the writers' methods, using appropriate subject terminology • Clear understanding of the effects of the writers' methods on the reader	• Clear understanding of ideas / perspectives / contextual factors shown by links made between these and the text / task

The key words are <u>clear</u> and <u>understanding</u>.

Sample Answer 1

I am going to compare 'Neutral Tones' with 'Winter Swans'. Both the poets are remembering being with their lover or wife out in the country in the winter. Hardy's memories are not happy at all and you get the impression the woman has left him and made him bitter but Sheers describes a happy ending to the walk.[1]

Hardy starts with a description of a dull day: 'the sun was white, as though chidden of God'. This sets a depressing mood, which might be how the poet is feeling. Sheers also describes the weather and the earth 'gulping for breath'.[2]

Sheers and his lover are 'silent and apart' as if they have had a row but he does not say what it was about. Hardy does talk to his lover but it is not pleasant. Her eyes are 'as eyes that rove over tedious riddles' as if she is trying to work him out. He describes her smile as 'the deadest thing'.[3] They really hate each other and whatever love they had has gone. Sheers does not describe the woman at all but whatever has gone wrong does not seem serious because when she tells him about the swans mating for life they hold hands and you feel they will be together forever like the swans.[4]

Both poems are in stanzas. Hardy's are very regular – four lines each with the same rhyme scheme. Sheers has more stanzas but they are only three lines each and the lines are different lengths. The last stanza is only two lines to show it is important.[5]

Both use imagery of nature to show how they feel. The winter weather gives the same sad mood in both. Hardy compares the woman to 'an ominous bird a-wing'. On the other hand, the swans in 'Winter Swans' are symbolic of faithfulness and love. They give hope to the couple whereas Hardy is left only with sad memories and bitterness.[6]

[1] Starts with an explained comparison, showing understanding of what the poems are about (AO1).

[2] A clear comparison, effectively supported by quotations from both poems. The comments about mood show some understanding of the writers' methods and their effect on the reader (AO1/AO2).

[3] Another clear comparison, well supported by integrated references to the texts (AO1).

[4] The comparison is becoming more developed, again supported by reference to the texts (AO1). Perhaps there is some understanding of implicit ideas shown here (AO3).

[5] Comments on structure, using relevant terminology, and an attempt to explain the writers' methods, but does not explain the effect of the writers' methods on the reader (AO2).

[6] Here the writers' use of imagery is explained quite clearly and understanding is shown of the effect on the reader (AO1/AO2).

- AO1: Comparisons are clear and understanding of the poems is shown clearly, so overall this is a Level 4 answer. Comparisons are sometimes developed so AO1 might just meet Level 5.
- AO2: Not as secure but there is some clear explanation of the writers' methods and their effects with relevant terminology used. (Level 4)
- AO3: Difficult to judge, partly because the examiners reward discussion of ideas where they feel an understanding of context is 'implied'. Here there is no explicit mention of context but a generous examiner might detect an implied understanding of ideas and perspectives. (Level 2 or 3)

On balance, a mark in the middle of Level 4 would be fair.

| Mark | 18 / 30 (Level 4, equivalent to approx. grade 5) |

To move this answer into Levels 5 and 6, the candidate needs to explore comparisons in more depth, making sure all points are supported with textual evidence, analyse the effects of the writers' methods using appropriate subject terminology, and explore ideas and perspectives in terms of context.

The exam board is looking for:

	AO1	AO2	AO3
Level 6	• Critical exploratory comparison • Judicious use of precise references to the texts	• Analysis of the writers' methods with subject terminology used judiciously • Exploration of the effect of the writers' methods on the reader	• Exploration of ideas / perspectives / contextual factors shown by specific detailed links between context and text / task

The key words are critical, analysis and exploration.

Sample Answer 2

Both 'Neutral Tones' and 'Winter Swans' focus on a single memory of an encounter with a lover. Both poems are set in winter, with the descriptions of the winter landscape setting a tone of bleak melancholy. However, the outcomes of their epiphanies are very different.[1]

Hardy starts with a description of a dull day: 'the sun was white, as though chidden of God'. The harshness of this phrase, suggesting a world without hope, sets the tone for the rest of the poem. The landscape is 'white' and 'gray' – the 'neutral tones' of the title – implying a lack of life and colour and reflecting the mood of the writer. Like Hardy, Sheers uses pathetic fallacy but he takes the device further, ascribing human qualities to the earth, which he describes as 'gulping for breath'. The onomatopoeic 'gulping' conveys both the sound of the mud as they wade through it and the apparently desperate state of the poet's relationship.[2]

Sheers and his lover are 'silent and apart' as if they have had a row but he does not say what it was about. Nor does Hardy give any details of what has driven him and his lover apart. However, there is a difference in their treatment of the women. While Sheers does not either describe his lover/wife or try to analyse her feelings, Hardy focuses on the woman in the second and third stanzas. Her eyes are 'as eyes that rove / over tedious riddles of years ago' and her words 'played'. This gives a sense of someone who knows him well but for whom their relationship has become a game or a joke. There are no feelings left. In the third stanza the nature of his feelings for her, as well as hers for him, becomes clear as he describes her smile as 'the deadest thing...a grin of bitterness'.[3]

There is no hope for Hardy's relationship and the memory of this incident returns to him whenever he thinks of the 'keen lessons' of love that have left him cynical. This memory of 'a pond edged with grayish leaves' has become a symbol of all that is wrong with love (and perhaps women), emphasised by the flatness of the rhythm and plainness of the words in a depressing final line. In contrast, Sheers tells us how his lover's remark about the swans mating for life leads to a gentle, almost casual reconciliation as they hold hands. Sheers's final line, comparing their hands to 'a pair of wings settling after flight' is gentle, understated and full of hope for their future together.[4]

'Neutral Tones' is structured like a ballad in regularly rhyming quatrains. This gives order to Hardy's story and his memories. 'Winter Swans' is also mainly regular in form but the lack of a strong rhythm and the use of enjambment, causing the first four and then the final three stanzas to flow seamlessly into each other, gives a more gentle, conversational feeling to the poem. The first full stop, coming at the end of the third stanza marks a change in the mood and the beginning of the couple's reconciliation. [5]

Both poets use imagery of nature to show how they feel, descriptions of the winter weather initially creating similar moods. Both use birds as symbols. Hardy uses the simile 'like an ominous bird a-wing' to alert us to the hopelessness of the situation. Sheers, on the other hand, turns the literal imagery of the swans into a powerful symbol of faithfulness and love. They give hope to the couple as they move on hand in hand, whereas Hardy in his final stanza comes full circle, returning to a memory that only brings sorrow and bitterness. [6]

[1] A thoughtful explained comparison, referring to the writers' methods and using appropriate subject terminology (AO1/AO2).

[2] A detailed comparison of the writers' methods and their effect on the reader, effectively supported by quotation from both poems (AO1/AO2).

[3] Another thoughtful comparison, supported by well-chosen references to the texts. Becoming exploratory in its consideration of ideas, with awareness of contextual factors implied (AO1/AO2/AO3).

[4] The comparison is now definitely exploratory and the use of references judicious (AO1). A thoughtful examination of the writers' methods in the consideration of their final lines (AO2). Again, shows understanding and consideration of ideas and perspectives (AO3).

[5] Analysis of structure and its effect, using subject terminology well, as the exploratory comparison continues (AO2).

[6] The writers' use of imagery and its effect on the reader are analysed as the candidate critically explores the writers' methods and perspectives (AO1/AO2/AO3).

- AO1: Comparisons are critical and exploratory, with precise and judicious reference to the text. (Level 6)
- AO2: Convincing analysis of the writers' methods throughout. Excellent use of subject terminology. (Level 6)
- AO3: Ideas and perspectives are explored thoughtfully but there is still a lack of detailed links between context and task. (Level 5)

Mark ▶ **28 / 30 (Level 6, equivalent to approx. grade 8)**

For more on the topics covered in this chapter, see pages 96–103 of the Collins AQA English Language & Literature Revision Guide.

The Exam

You should aim to spend no more than 45 minutes on the Unseen Poetry section of Paper 2 (Section C).

There will be two unseen poems printed on the question paper and two questions. The first question will be about the first poem only and will be worth 24 marks. The second question will ask you to compare both poems and is worth 8 marks.

Skills Assessed in the Poetry Section

This section assesses your ability to analyse poems that you have never seen before, using the skills that you have learned in class through studying the poetry anthology.

You will be assessed on Assessment Objectives 1 and 2 only. Because the poems will be new to you, it will not be possible to discuss context (AO3). For the second question the focus is entirely on comparison but the mark scheme is still based on AO1 and AO2. For details of the AOs, see page 68.

It may seem odd to have a separate, short question comparing the two poems when you have already analysed one in detail. The reason for it seems to be that the exam board wants to / is obliged to give a certain percentage of overall marks in English Literature for comparison. Make sure that you do not run out of time before you reach question 2. If you allow yourself 10–15 minutes, you should be able to pick up 7 or 8 marks without too much trouble.

Question 1

Approaching an Unseen Poem

Start by reading the poem quickly to get a general idea of its themes and style. Then read it more carefully, highlighting words and phrases that strike you as worth commenting on. You should now be 'interrogating' the text, using your knowledge of poetry to ask questions about the poem. You might consider these things:

The title	• What does it make you think about? • Does it clearly state what the poem is about or is it **ambiguous**?
Voice and audience	• Who is the speaker and what do you learn about him/her? • Who, if anyone, is being addressed and why?
What happens	• Does the poem tell a story and, if so, what is it? • Is it about an event (an epiphany perhaps) that changes things for the poet/speaker? • Or is it just about the poet's feelings without any narrative?
Settings	• Is it set at a particular time, a period in history or a time in the poet's past? • Does the time change? • Is it set in a place and, if so, what sort of place? • Does the place change?
Form and structure	• How is the poem organised? • If it is in stanzas, when and why does the poet start a new stanza? • Is there a regular rhythm and can you clearly identify the metre? • What is the effect of its regularity/irregularity? • Are there any changes in the regular pattern, for example changes in stanza or line length? If so, what is their effect? • Does the poet use **enjambment** and, if so, when and why? • Does the poem rhyme and is there a regular rhyme scheme? • What is the effect of any rhyme (including internal rhyme and half rhyme) used?
Language	• How does the poem use sounds and to what effect? • What sort of imagery is used and what is its effect? • Is there anything else that strikes you as interesting about the language used?
Themes and ideas	• What do you think the poem is really about? • Are there any other ideas present? • What is the poet's attitude to his/her themes?
Your response	• How does the poem make you, as a reader, feel and react?

Not all these questions will be relevant to the poem and you may not be able to cover every aspect of the poem in the time available. However, they provide a useful starting point for analysis.

> ### Top Tip
>
> Be confident about offering your interpretation but bear in mind that the poem you are given is unlikely to be obscure or difficult. Your response is as valid as anyone else's.
>
> During revision, practise analysing poems you have not read before. At first you could use the checklist on page 131 for guidance, before moving on to practice in exam conditions. You could use poems from the section of the anthology you have not studied.

Worked Example

See page 3 for suggestions on how to make effective use of the worked example.

Elegy   *D H Lawrence*

Since I lost you, my darling, the sky has come near,
And I am of it, the small sharp stars are quite near,
The white moon going among them like a white bird among snow-berries,
And the sound of her gently rustling in heaven like a bird I hear.

And I am willing to come to you now, my dear,   5
As a pigeon lets itself off from a cathedral dome
To be lost in the haze of the sky, I would like to come,
And be lost out of sight with you, and be gone like foam.

For I am tired, my dear, and if I could lift my feet,
My tenacious feet from off the dome of the earth   10
To fall like a breath within the breathing wind
Where you are lost, what rest, my love, what rest!

1 In 'Elegy' how does the poet present the speaker's feelings about the death of a loved one? [24 marks]

The question reminds you to write about the writer's methods by using the words <u>how</u> and <u>present</u>. It also gives you the focus of both the poem and your answer in terms of its main theme – 'the death of a loved one'. The term 'elegy' is used to describe a poem to or about someone who has died.

Among the things that might strike you immediately are:

- the speaker directly addresses the person who has died
- the words 'darling' and 'dear' suggest he could be addressing a wife or lover
- he feels both love and grief very intensely, writing about his feelings rather than about her as a person, so it could apply to anyone in that situation
- he seems to want to die to be with her
- there are three stanzas of four lines (quatrains) but the lines are not of even length and there is no strong, regular rhythm
- he uses natural imagery to express his feelings
- there is ambiguity in his attitude – does he see her as living on somewhere or is death just nothingness?

To get a reasonably good mark (Level 4, equivalent to grade 4–5 or above), you need the following:

	AO1	AO2
Level 4 13–16 marks	• Clear explained response to the task • Effective use of references to support explanation	• Clear explanation of the writers' methods, using appropriate subject terminology • Clear understanding of the effects of the writers' methods on the reader

The key words are <u>clear</u> and <u>understanding</u>.

Sample Answer 1

The speaker is talking to someone who has died. He thinks she is in the sky and he wants to be with her.[1]

He tells her that the 'sky has come near' and so have the stars and the moon. Then he says he wants to 'come to you'[2] and there is a simile about being a pigeon that flies from a cathedral dome and gets lost in the sky. He says he wants to get lost too and be 'out of sight' which I think means he wants to be dead too.[3]

He says he is tired so he might be old and that is why he is ready to die. He keeps calling the person 'love' and 'darling' so he must love them very much. He wants to be with her and he sees it as a rest.[4]

> *I think it is a very sad poem and a reader who has lost someone might feel that they have the same feelings that D H Lawrence has put into words.*[5]

[1] Basic statements showing some understanding of the subject matter (AO1) with a reference to the poet's methods (AO2).

[2] Uses a few quotations but they do not really support comments/explanations, just repeating what is in the poem (AO1).

[3] Identifies the writer's use of a literary technique, using subject terminology and explains it clearly (AO2).

[4] A better attempt at explaining what the poem is about, supported by references (AO1).

[5] A personal response that shows understanding of the effect of the poem on the reader but doesn't tie the response to the writer's methods (AO1/AO2).

- AO1: The response to the poem is explained clearly at times and references are used to support the comments. The question for an examiner would be whether there is just 'some' response, which would be Level 3, or enough for Level 4. The references do 'support a range of relevant comments' (Level 3) but are they used effectively (Level 4)? (Borderline Level 4)
- AO2: There are relevant comments on the writer's methods and their effect on the reader but there is not enough clear explanation of them for Level 4. (Level 3)

Overall, the answer achieves the top of Level 3 and has just enough clear explanation and understanding to reach the bottom of Level 4.

| Mark | 13 / 24 (Level 4, equivalent to approx. grade 4) |

To improve the answer, you need a lot more detailed analysis, better use of references and subject terminology, and a developed exploration of the poem and its effect on the reader.

A top Level 6 answer, equivalent to grade 8–9, requires the following:

	AO1	AO2
Level 6 21–24 marks	• Critical, exploratory conceptualised response to the task and text • Judicious use of precise references to support interpretation	• Analysis of the writers' methods, using subject terminology judiciously • Exploration of the effects of the writers' methods on the reader

The key words are <u>analysis</u> and <u>exploration</u>.

Sample Answer 2

In keeping with the title, the poem is about the speaker's grief for a loved one who has died. He speaks directly to her and we get the impression she was his wife or lover from the use of the affectionate terms 'my darling' and 'my dear'.[1]

In the first stanza he uses natural imagery to express how his world has changed since the death: 'The sky has come near / and I am of it'. He could be playing with the idea of the dead being in Heaven (which is often described as being beyond the sky) because he then refers to 'heaven', which could be taken as referring to the sky or to the religious concept of life after death. His grief seems to have made him intensely aware of nature. He uses a simile to compare the moon to 'a white bird among snow-berries', using natural imagery to describe nature. The moon is personified as female, the repetition of 'white' emphasising its traditional association with purity. Perhaps the moon 'gently rustling in heaven' represents the loved one.[2]

In the second stanza the poet describes what his grief makes him want to do. He moves from being 'willing to come', suggesting he would accept death, to 'I would like to come'. This stronger statement implies that he might be thinking of suicide. Again, he uses a simile about a bird, this time to describe himself. Unlike the 'white bird among snow-berries' the pigeon on the cathedral roof suggests something down-to-earth and not that attractive, part of an ordinary mundane existence. He repeats a desire to be 'lost', though this is rather contradicted by adding 'out of sight with you'. The phrase 'gone like foam' also suggests ambiguity about death. If he were 'gone like foam' he would be in a state of nothingness, suggesting the lover is too, yet he speaks to her as if she still exists.[3]

The final stanza explains his desire for death: 'for I am tired'. This suggests less of a positive desire to kill himself and more of a willingness to accept the inevitability of death. He says that his feet are 'tenacious', suggesting his body is not ready to die even if his spirit is (he may be old but healthy). He brings back the idea of the 'dome', now applying it to the earth and, by implication, life itself.[4]

The final two lines suggest that life continues after death in some way. She is 'lost' but she is part of 'the breathing wind'. It is a gentle ending to a poem of intense grief and the final exclamation of 'what rest, my love, what rest!' suggests that he is reconciled to the idea of death, feeling that he will be reunited with his love. [5]

[1] Clear explanation showing understanding of the subject matter, supported by quotation (AO1) and a consideration of the use of language (AO2).

[2] A very thoughtful, exploratory analysis of the poet's feelings and methods, very well supported by precise references to the text (AO1/AO2).

[3] The thoughtful, exploratory approach continues, rooted firmly in the text as the candidate considers possible ambiguities. It is now certainly 'critical' as required in Level 4 (AO1/AO2).

[4] The answer is firmly in the top level by now, the critical approach being sustained and references used judiciously (AO1/AO2).

[5] A good conclusion, giving a personal response that shows understanding and appreciation of the effect of the poem on the reader (AO1/AO2).

- AO1: A critical, exploratory response with an excellent use of well-chosen references throughout. (Level 6)
- AO2: Language is analysed perceptively throughout and subject terminology used accurately, with the effect of the writer's methods being explored. There is not much, if any, analysis of form and structure. The top of Level 6 does ask for this but, given that there is a limit to how much can be covered in the time, this is not a major drawback. (Level 6)

Mark ▶ **23 / 24 (Level 6, equivalent to approx. grade 9)**

Question 2

Comparing Two Unseen Poems

For this question you will be given a second unseen poem, which you will have to compare to the one you have already commented on.

Although this question does not carry many marks, it can be tricky. The examiners' mark scheme states that marks can only be awarded for comparisons, so everything you say about the second poem must be related to the first one. As you have already written about the first poem, it is inevitable that you will re-use some of the same material. Do not worry about this – just make sure that your comments are tied to those about the second poem.

For example, if you have said in answer to question 1…

The poet uses the second person to address a loved one who has died.

…you can still say:

Both poets use the second person to address someone directly. However, the first poet is a bereaved person addressing someone who has died while the voice of the second poem is the dead person addressing the bereaved.

Remember to comment on both similarities and differences.

> **Top Tip**
>
> If you have not finished the first question on the unseen poetry and have only 10–15 minutes left, leave it and do the second part. You are unlikely to add many marks towards the end of a long answer, but you could easily gain 7 or 8 from a brief but perceptive comparison.

For more guidance on comparing poems, see pages 123–129.

Worked Example

Remember   *Christina Rossetti*

Remember me when I am gone away,
Gone far away into the silent land;
When you can no more hold me by the hand,
Nor I half turn to go yet turning stay.
Remember me when no more day by day   5
You tell me of our future that you planned:
Only remember me; you understand
It will be late to counsel then or pray.
Yet if you should forget me for a while
And afterwards remember, do not grieve: 10
For if the darkness and corruption leave
A vestige of the thoughts that once I had,
Better by far you should forget and smile
Than that you should remember and be sad.

2 In 'Elegy' and 'Remember' the poets write about how the death of a loved one affects people. What are the similarities and/or differences between the ways in which the poets describe these feelings?   [8 marks]

To achieve Level 3, equivalent to grade 5–6, you need the following:

	AO2
Level 3 5–6 marks	• Thoughtful comparison of the writers' use of language and/or structure and/or form, supported by effective use of subject terminology • Comparative examination of the effects of the writers' methods on the reader

Below Level 3, you only need 'relevant' comparison and use of subject terminology, and some comparison of the effects of the writers' methods.

Sample Answer 1

Both poets use 'you'. In 'Elegy' the poet talks to someone he loves who has died but in 'Remember' it is the dead person talking to someone and telling them not to be too sad.[1]

Rossetti tells someone she loves to remember her 'when you can no more hold me by the hand'. She does not want him to 'pray' for her because it will be too late and she does not seem to mind if sometimes he does forget her. She wants him to get on with his life and not be too sad.[2]

'Remember' is written in one stanza, like a sonnet, which is a love poem, whereas 'Elegy' is broken up into three stanzas. You know he loves the person because he calls her 'darling'. There is rhyme in both poems.[3]

Both poems are sad but Rossetti is telling her loved one that everything is all right whether he remembers her or not. Lawrence does not want to forget the lover but wants to be with her. If you read the second poem you might feel better about getting on with your life but the first one does not make you think it will be better till you die.[4]

[1] This is a relevant comparison of the writers' use of language but the comments are not developed enough to be 'thoughtful'.
[2] There is no comparison here so this paragraph would be ignored by the marker.
[3] A comparison of form and structure, using relevant subject terminology. The reference to sonnet form might be considered thoughtful.

[4] A comparative examination of the effects of the writers' methods on the reader, although the comments are not tied specifically to aspects of language, form or structure.

There are relevant comparisons made here and they are supported by some relevant use of subject terminology. There is also some comparison of the effects of the writers' methods on the reader. This answer fulfils the requirements for Level 2. It would probably just squeeze into Level 3.

Mark ▸ **5 / 8 (Level 3, equivalent to approx. grade 5)**

A Level 4 answer, equivalent to grades 8–9, requires the following:

	AO2
Level 4 7–8 marks	• Exploratory comparison of the writers' use of language, supported by judicious use of subject terminology • Convincing comparison of the effects of the writers' methods on the reader

The key words are exploratory and convincing.

This mark scheme does not mention reference to the text but examples given by the exam board make it clear that you are expected to make relevant references to both poems.

Sample Answer 2

Both poets use the second person, 'you', to address someone directly. However, while in 'Elegy' the voice is that of a bereaved person addressing someone he loves who has died, conversely in 'Remember' the speaker talks to a loved one about how to react when she is dead.[1]

While 'Remember' follows strictly the traditional form of a sonnet, with fourteen lines and a regular iambic pentameter, 'Elegy' is less regular, including some variation in line length as the poet's grief gets the better of him, particularly in the third line of the first stanza. There is a volta in 'Remember' from line 8 to line 9. She moves from urging him to remember her to telling him it does not matter if he does not remember. The mood turns to a gentler, more accepting one. Lawrence too seems to control his grief more and becomes more accepting as he moves through the stanzas, although there is no great change in his feelings.[2]

Rossetti speaks of death as being 'far away into the silent land'. This is similar to Lawrence's idea of his lover being 'lost out of sight'. They both use metaphors that imply that they think of death as not being the end. The difference is in the attitude to bereavement rather than death itself. Lawrence wants to 'be gone like foam' and longs for 'rest', seeing the only way out of his sorrow as death. Rossetti does not want this for her lover, telling him not to 'grieve' or 'be sad' and saying that she only wants him to be happy when he remembers her.[3]

This practical, sensible attitude is reflected in Rossetti's language as she remembers everyday things like when he would 'hold me by the hand' or 'tell me of our future'. Lawrence, in contrast, does not give an idea of life with his lover, instead using rich imagery to express his feelings of grief. Readers of 'Elegy' who have been bereaved might feel great empathy with the speaker but he does not offer hope or an end to grief in this world. 'Remember', on the other hand, might give comfort as it seems to be giving the reader permission to move on and be happy: 'Better by far you should forget and smile'.[4]

[1] This is a better, more accurate and thoughtful comparison of the writers' methods.

[2] A detailed exploration of the poets' use of form and structure supported by appropriate subject terminology and helpful references to the texts.

[3] A convincing comparison of the effects of the writers' use of language on the reader. Good use of supporting quotations.

[4] Further thoughtful and exploratory comparative examination of the effects of the writers' methods on the reader.

This answer is a convincing comparison of the two poems. It does not cover every aspect of the poems in detail, but this would be impossible in the time available. The examiners would not expect anything better than this.

Mark 8 / 8 (Level 4, equivalent to approx. grade 8–9)

For more on the topics covered in this chapter, see pages 104–105 of the Collins AQA English Language & Literature Revision Guide.

active voice when the subject is the person or thing doing an action, e.g. the dog bit the boy

allegory a story with a second (metaphorical) meaning, partly hidden by its literal meaning

alliteration repetition of a consonant sound in two or more words, especially at the start of each word

ambiguity (adj. *ambiguous*) having more than one meaning (sometimes deliberately)

anapaest two unstressed syllables followed by a stressed syllable

anaphora the repetition of a word or phrase at intervals, usually at the beginning of a line or sentence

anecdote (adj. *anecdotal*) a short account of an interesting or humorous story, often used to reinforce a point being made

aside a line or lines addressed to the audience while other actors are on stage

assonance repetition of a vowel sound within words

autobiographical writing any writing about the author's own experiences

autobiography the story of the author's life

ballad a form of poetry that tells a story, usually in quatrains with a regular rhythm and rhyme scheme

bathos (adj. *bathetic*) an unintended lapse into the ridiculous

Bildungsroman a novel that tells the story of someone growing up

biography (adj. *biographical*) the story of someone's life

blank verse poetry that has a regular metre but does not rhyme

Brechtian in the style or using the techniques of the playwright Bertolt Brecht, usually denoting a breaking with naturalistic conventions (also known as the 'alienation effect')

caesura a pause in a line of poetry, usually indicated by a punctuation mark

chronological order in order of time, starting with the earliest event

clause a phrase (group of words) that could stand alone as a sentence; having a main verb

climax the dramatic high point of a story, usually near the end

colloquial (noun *colloquialism*) conversational or chatty

complex sentence a sentence containing more than one clause (but not a compound sentence)

compound sentence two clauses of equal value joined by 'and', 'or' or 'but'

conceit an elaborate or far-fetched simile or extended metaphor

connotation a meaning suggested by a word or phrase

dactyl one stressed syllable followed by two unstressed syllables

denouement the 'untying' or explanation of the complications of a plot towards the end of a novel, story or play

dialect words or phrases particular to a regional variety of English

diction the choice of words and phrases used

direct address speaking directly to the audience, usually using 'you'

direct speech the actual words spoken, put in inverted commas

discourse marker a word or phrase that connects sentences or paragraphs

dramatic monologue a long poem in which a character speaks to the reader or audience

emotive language language used to provoke emotions, such as shock or pity, in a reader

enjambment when lines are not end-stopped with a punctuation mark but the sense runs on between lines or stanzas

epiphany a moment of revelation or insight

eponymous adjective applied to the person after whom a work is named, e.g. Jane Eyre.

exposition setting a scene or giving background information at the beginning of a story

fable a story, often about animals, that gives a moral lesson

figurative imagery the use of an image of one thing to tell us about another

fourth wall the convention in naturalistic theatre that there is an invisible wall between the actors and the audience

fragment another word for a minor sentence (i.e. one that does not contain a main verb)

free indirect discourse (or free indirect style) a way of presenting the thoughts and feelings of a character from that character's point of view by combining features of direct and indirect discourse. For example, if direct discourse (like direct speech) were: *I will propose tomorrow,' he thought*, then indirect discourse would be: *He thought that he would propose on the following day.* Free indirect discourse might be: *He would propose tomorrow.*

free verse poetry that does not have a regular metre or rhyme scheme

genre a kind/type of literature, e.g. detective story or travel writing

Gothic usually applied to stories of suspense and terror, sometimes said to be a populist form of Romanticism

half rhyme an imperfect rhyme in which the final consonants of a line agree but the vowels do not; also known as near rhyme, slant rhyme and pararhyme

hyperbole exaggeration

iamb an unstressed syllable followed by a stressed syllable

iambic pentameter verse in which each line has five iambs

idiolect a way of speaking that is peculiar to an individual person

image a picture, also used metaphorically of 'word pictures'

imagery when words are so descriptive that they paint a picture in your mind

inciting incident an event that starts the action of a story

indirect speech speech that is reported rather than quoted; also called 'reported speech'

infer (noun *inference*) to deduce something that is not openly stated

intrusive narrator a narrator who is not part of the action but comments on it

irony (adj. *ironic*) when words are used to imply an opposite meaning, or sarcastic language that can be used to mock or convey scorn

juxtaposition the placing of two words, phrases or ideas next to each other. The use of the term does **not** imply opposition or contrast

literal imagery the use of description to convey mood or atmosphere

lyric poetry short poems expressing personal moods or feelings

metaphor an image created by directly comparing one thing to another, e.g. 'my brother is a little monkey'

metre the pattern of stressed and unstressed syllables in poetry

minor sentence a sentence that does not contain a verb; sometimes called a '**fragment**'

motif an idea or image that is repeated at intervals in a text

myth (adj. *mythical*) a story, usually traditional, containing deep truths about life, often with religious significance in a culture

naïve narrator a narrator who does not understand what is happening, often a child

naturalism (adj. *naturalistic*) (in theatre) an imitation of life through realistic sets, costumes, dialogue and acting

onomatopoeia the use of a word that sounds like what it describes

omniscient narrator a narrator who is outside the action and knows everything

oxymoron two contradictory words placed together, e.g. 'bitter sweet'

paraphrase to put something into your own words

pararhyme another word for half rhyme

parentheses (singular *parenthesis*) brackets; a word or phrase inserted into a sentence to explain something

passive voice where the subject has the action done to him or her, e.g. the boy was bitten by the dog

pathetic fallacy either a form of personification (giving nature human qualities) or the use of a description of surroundings to reflect a character's mood

persona a fictional voice used by a poet

personification when an inanimate object or idea is given human qualities, e.g. 'the television stared at me across the room'

Petrarchan (or Italian) **sonnet** a form of sonnet consisting of an octave and a sestet

polemic a written attack on an idea or policy

protagonist the main character; the person whom the story is about

quatrain a set of four lines of verse

register the form of language used in particular circumstances

rhetoric (adj. *rhetorical*) the art of speaking, especially to persuade

rhetorical device a language technique used to influence an audience

rhetorical question a question that does not require an answer, which is used to make readers think about the possible answer and involve them in the text

rhyme the use of words with the same endings to make patterns

rhyming couplet two successive lines of poetry that rhyme

Romanticism (adj. *Romantic*) a literary movement of the early 19th century that focused on the freedom of individual expression; it is associated with intense personal feelings, a love of nature and the use of traditional forms

satire writing that criticises people or society through humour

scansion (verb *scan*) the analysis of poetic metre in verse lines

sibilance repetition of 's' sounds

simile a comparison of one thing to another using the words 'like' or 'as', e.g. 'the raindrops fell like tears'

simple sentence a sentence that only contains a main clause

slang informal language, often regional and/or changing quickly

slant rhyme see half rhyme

soliloquy a speech to the audience expressing a character's thoughts or feelings

sonnet a form of poem, usually a love poem of 14 lines

spondee two stressed syllables, occasionally used as a substitute for an iamb or a trochee

Standard English the variety of English generally accepted as the correct form for writing and formal speech

stanza a section of a poem, often called a verse

stress (in poetry) emphasis

subordinate clause a clause that gives extra information

syllable a unit of pronunciation

symbol (adj. *symbolic*) an object that represents something else, e.g. an idea or emotion

trochee a stressed syllable followed by an unstressed syllable

unreliable narrator a narrator who cannot always be trusted

volta a turn or change in a poem, especially between the octave and sestet in a Petrarchan sonnet

Acknowledgements

The author and publisher are grateful to the copyright holders for permission to use quoted materials and images.

Page 1: © wavebreakmedia/Shutterstock.com
Pages 7, 8 & 12: *Nineteen Eighty-Four* by George Orwell (Copyright © George Orwell, 1949), by permission of Bill Hamilton as the Literary Executor of the Estate of the Late Sonia Brownell Orwell.
Ebook usage: *Nineteen Eighty-Four* by George Orwell (Penguin Books, 2004). Copyright © Eric Blair, 1949. This edition copyright © The Estate of the late Sonia Brownell Orwell, 1987.
Page 35: ©Lee Morriss/Shutterstock.com
Page 43: With thanks to The National Library of Wales
Page 115: 'Walking Away' from *Selected Poems* by Cecil Day Lewis, reprinted by permission of Peters Fraser & Dunlop (www.petersfraserdunlop.com) on behalf of the Estate of Cecil Day Lewis.
Pages 116 & 121: 'Remains' was taken from: *The Not Dead*, by Simon Armitage, © Simon Armitage. Published by Pomona Books. Used by kind permission of Pomona Books.
Page 121: 'Singh Song!' from *Look We Have Coming to Dover!* by Daljit Nagra. Copyright © 2007 Faber & Faber
Page 121: 'Follower' from *Death of a Naturalist* by Seamus Heaney. Copyright © 1966 Faber & Faber.

Published by Collins
An imprint of HarperCollins*Publishers*
1 London Bridge Street
London SE1 9GF

ISBN: 978-0-00-822738-8
First published 2017
10 9 8 7 6 5 4 3 2 1
© HarperCollins*Publishers* Limited 2017

Commissioning Editors: Katherine Wilkinson and Clare Souza
Author: Paul Burns
Project Management and Editorial: Richard Toms and Alissa McWhinnie
Cover Design: Sarah Duxbury
Inside Concept Design: Paul Oates
Text Design and Layout: QBS Learning
Production: Natalia Rebow
Printed and bound in China by RR Donnelley APS